Color Mixing Recipes

FOR LANDSCAPES

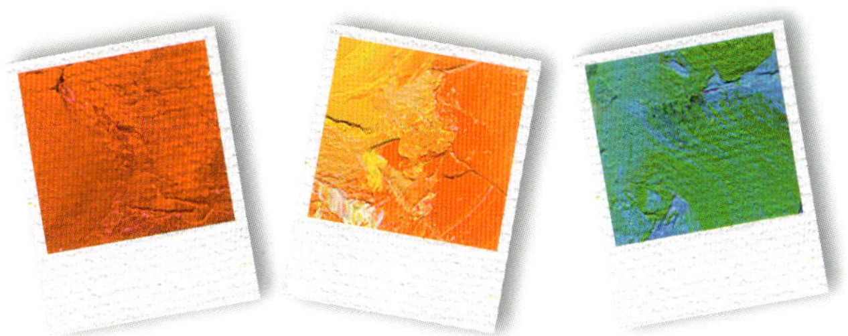

Mixing Recipes for More Than 500 Color Combinations

BY WILLIAM F. POWELL

Quarto.com • WalterFoster.com

First published in 2017 by Walter Foster Publishing, an imprint of The Quarto Group.
100 Cummings Center, Suite 265D, Beverly, MA 01915, USA.
T (978) 282-9590 **F** (978) 283-2742

EEA Representation, WTS Tax d.o.o.,
Žanova ulica 3, 4000 Kranj, Slovenia.
www.wts-tax.si

Walter Foster Publishing titles are also available at discount for retail, wholesale, promotional, and bulk purchase. For details, contact the Special Sales Manager by email at specialsales@quarto.com or by mail at The Quarto Group, Attn: Special Sales Manager, 100 Cummings Center, Suite 265D, Beverly, MA 01915, USA.

ISBN: 978-1-60058-266-0

Printed in Guangdong, China TT012026
15 14

Contents

INCLUDES MORE THAN 1,500 SUBJECTS AND SUB-ELEMENTS

- Flowers: numerous varieties
- Mountains: base, shadows, highlights, and hazes
- Rocks: various geological types
- Sands, clays, and gravels
- Sea, ocean, surf, foam, and fog
- Shadows: warm, cool, and various grays and purples
- Skies and clouds: various times of day and night; also mood skies & stormy gray skies
- Snow: warm light, cool light, sunlit, and shadowed
- Soils: various types
- Stones and pebbles
- Sunlight source colors: time of day color control
- Trees: foliage and trunk colors for numerous broadleaf and coniferous varieties including bark and trunk texture
- Wildlife, animals, and birds: recipes for many species

Instructions

Color Mixing Recipes for Landscapes is a convenient reference book that holds 530 individual color mixes to help you achieve accurate and vibrant landscape paintings. This collection of color mixing recipes is unique in that it contains color mixtures pertaining to specific subjects and elements in the landscape, along with several hundred other supporting color recipes.

The Color Guidance Index (pages 38–47) features more than 1,500 subjects and sub-elements for painting landscapes. To use this book, first find the subject you would like to paint in the index and locate the corresponding color mixture or mixtures. Some subjects—such as skies, clouds, trees, and mountains—are broken down into species or types with sub-elements. For instance, the subject Trees is broken down into species with sub-elements of Foliage (dark, medium, and light colors) and Bark (basic, secondary, dark, and light colors), along with descriptions of the bark texture. Because of this unique subject presentation, some areas of the index do not appear in alphabetical order; instead, they are presented in the order in which an artist would use the colors to paint the subject as a whole.

IMPORTANT: Paint colors vary somewhat among brands, and even though extreme care was taken in the production of this book, slight variations in printing may occur. Nevertheless, if you use the color samples as a general guide, follow the recipes, and use accurate paint measurements, you will achieve great success in mixing beautiful colors.

PAINT COLORS

You will need all of the following colors to create all of the color mixing recipes in this book. Note: Some acrylic color names will vary depending on the manufacturer; also, some of these colors are not available in acrylic, so they must be mixed. Please refer to the Acrylic Color Conversion Chart on the inside front cover of this book, where we have also included oil color alternatives where possible.

Alizarin crimson
Burnt sienna
Burnt umber
Cadmium orange
Cadmium red light
Cadmium vermilion
Cadmium yellow medium
Cerulean blue hue
Cobalt blue
Cobalt violet hue
Ivory black
Magenta
Naples yellow hue
Permanent blue
Permanent green light
Raw sienna
Raw umber
Thalo® blue
Thalo® green (blue shade)
Thalo® red rose
Titanium white
Venetian red
Viridian green
Yellow ochre
Zinc yellow hue

USING THE MIXING GRID

Use the plastic Color Mixing Grid to measure the paint for each recipe. Use each square as one part and squeeze the paint out in uniform widths and lengths according to the formula. Some colors are so strong that only a minute amount is required to alter the color. When these colors are called for, the measurement in the recipe (which is about the size of a large pinhead) is referred to as a "speck" with a dot •.

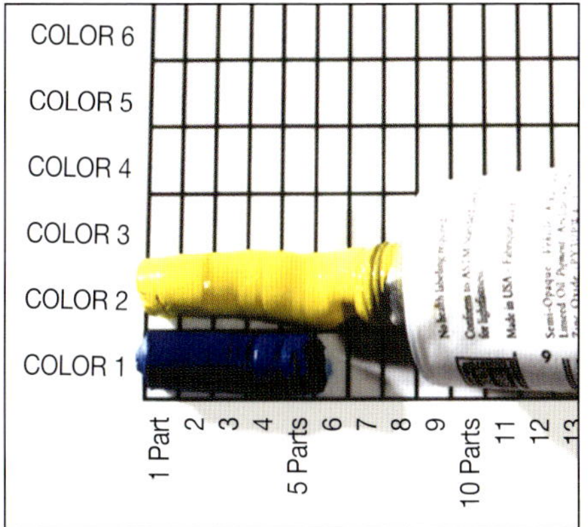

The **Color Mixing Grid** can also be used to measure the paint for your own color mixtures. Make notations of the quanity of each color you use so you can repeat the mixtures in the future.

Tip: Keep your mixtures simple. Don't mix too many different colors together because the color may become "muddy." However, even muddy colors are beautiful when used properly.

Mix freely and enjoy these color recipes! Use the **Color Mixing Grid** and create some color combinations of your own.

UsingTheRecipes

SKIES AND CLOUDS

The sky is the most important element in a painting because it influences the entire landscape composition, controlling the light, time of day, season, weather, color palette, and mood of a scene. Colors and lighting also vary in terms of color temperature, with the palette leaning either warm or cool. Early morning light is cooler than mid-afternoon or a warm evening sunset. Because of this, we use different color combinations and palettes for each skyscape. Different cloud formations also dictate weather and sky moods.

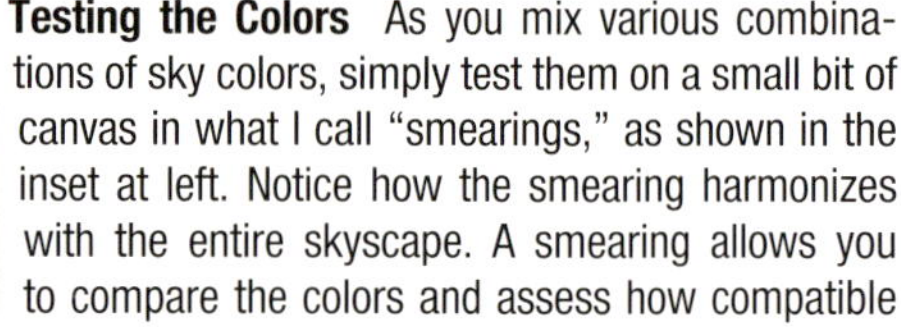

Testing the Colors As you mix various combinations of sky colors, simply test them on a small bit of canvas in what I call "smearings," as shown in the inset at left. Notice how the smearing harmonizes with the entire skyscape. A smearing allows you to compare the colors and assess how compatible each is with the others. You will find the recipes for this little color sketch in the index under "Daybreak Pinkish Sky." The color recipes used in this little painting are as follows: zenith #67, secondary color #68, and horizon colors #69 and #65. The clouds are as follows: main color #72, highlight colors #65 and #74, and shadow color #70.

Comparing Sky Moods The three small color sketches on this page are similar in composition and cloud formations. However, the time of day and color mood is completely different in each. Compare them and notice the difference.

Finding Recipes Complete recipes for the color sketches below are in the index under "Daybreak Blue Sky" (A) and "Dusk Blue Sky" (B). Index recipes range from daybreak to sunsets along with moonlight, stormy skies, and many other mood combinations. You can create complete, detailed paintings of any size using these color recipes.

Another method of using the color recipe swatches and index is to simply scan through the pages of recipe mixtures. Compare the swatches to the colors you see in your photo or subject. Select the dominant colors first, and then use the book to search for secondary and subtle color tones seen throughout your composition. Make notes and smearings of recipes you are considering to make certain they work well together. Create small non-detailed color sketches, such as the examples on these two pages. Once you have selected your colors, you can create a larger painting with great success.

A

B

Below are several sky mood sketches. The index name of each sketch is listed beneath. Select the one in the index that you would like to paint and follow the corresponding recipe numbers. The four thumbnail color sketches below are shown at the exact size they were painted.

Index: Early Morning Cool Sky with Clouds

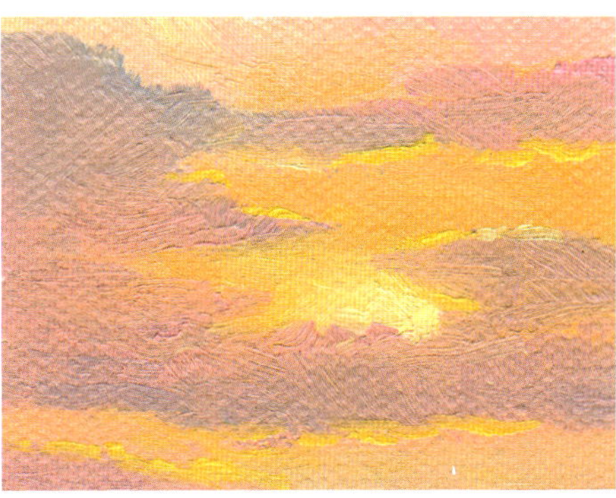

Index: Sunset Reddish Sky with Clouds

Index: Afternoon Warm Sky with Clouds

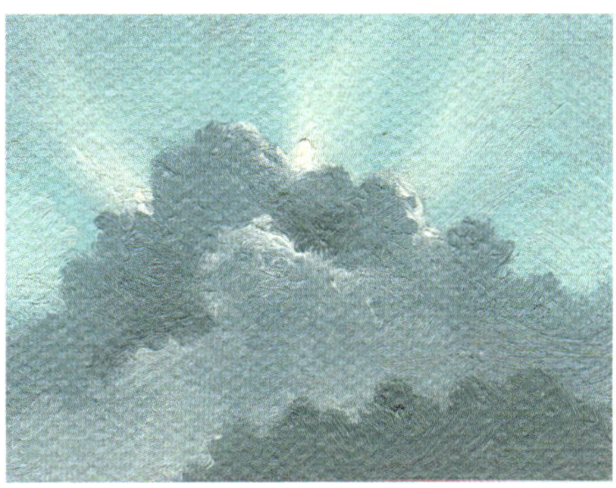

Index: Evening Sky, Clouds, and Light Rays

The rough color sketch of the desert rock below shows the versatility of using color recipes from different parts of the book to create a composition. The mood involves a warm, low light source on the desert red rock. Color recipes used in this sketch include the following:

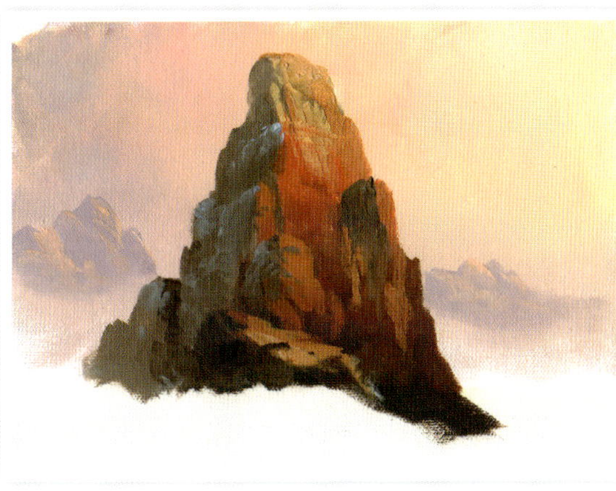

Sky: Begin at right and blend color mixtures toward the left. Start with #65 blended into #117 blended into #120.

Distant Rocks: Base color is #120 with highlights of #105. Main Rock: Paint the dark base shape using #43. Then add progressively lighter areas using recipes #22, #57, #30, #55, #18, and #40. Use a bit of #49 and #106 on the shadowed side. These mixes can be used to create any number of desert or seascape scenes with dramatic mood lighting. Remember to build colors from dark to light in this sketch.

Using The Recipes

OBSERVING COLORS IN NATURE

When we think of colors in nature, we usually say that skies are blue, trees are green, and so on. However, when we look closely and analyze the colors in an object, we find that not only does it contain a variety of color tones, but each object also contains a number of color **values** (the lightness or darkness of a color) within it.

Painting Trees When we look at a tree, our first impression is that it is made up of one overall color: green. Upon closer observation, we find it is made up of numerous tones of greens; several are a basic mass color, a secondary lighter color, a dark shadow color, and a highlight color. In some instances there are additional subtle values within the tree mass. This variation in color tones is what allows the artist to create the illusion of form and dimension within an object on a flat painting surface. All objects in nature are made up of a number of color tones, whether a tree trunk, rock, or mountain. Even a small leaf contains numerous tones. The simple example at right shows how the recipes for a coniferous tree have been selected and applied to develop a very realistic tree.

Compare the recipe colors used to paint the pine tree at right, and you will see how easily you can use the index to find the colors of the subject and then paint it using those colors.

You can also just scan through the mixtures and select colors you see in your subject. Below is a broadleaf bough that has been created using some of the same color mixtures used on the coniferous tree, plus a few added mixtures for warmth.

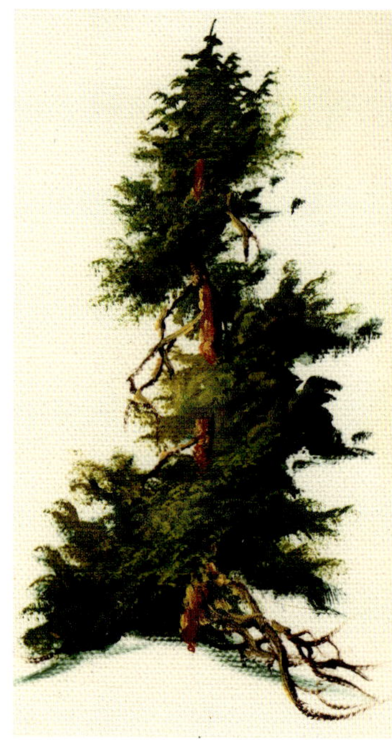

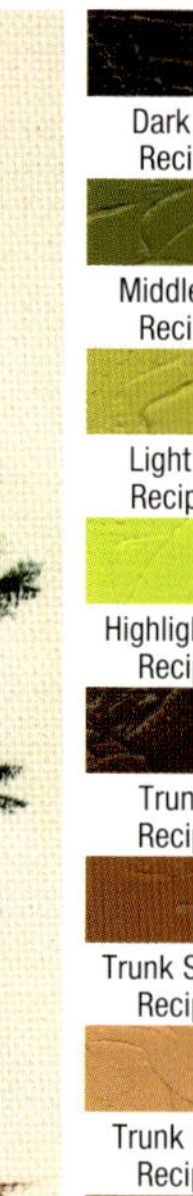

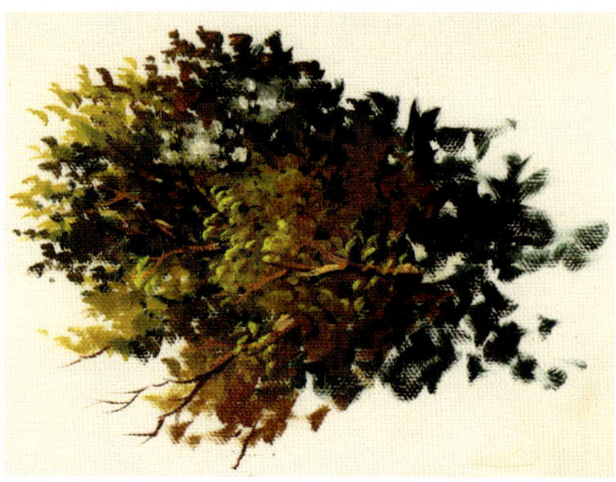

Broadleaf Bough Foliage: Dark green #81, secondary green #83, light green #95, highlight green #85, bright light green #87. Branches: Dark #43, secondary #55, and highlight #40.

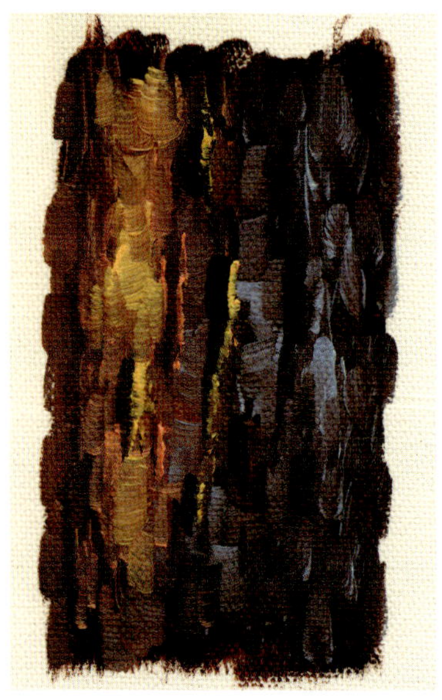

◀ **Pine Tree Trunk** Dark brown #43, secondary warm #48, middle light #59, highlight #40, and #141 for the cool accent color used within the shadow on the right side.

Tip: In all exercises, allow your brushstrokes and colors to blend into one another to create realistic form.

USING RECIPES TO PAINT MOUNTAINS

There are many types and colors of mountains, but one of the most common is gray. This entire exercise uses only recipe mixes from this book. Below you can see how easily you can create an entire scene using the recipes. Go to the index and find "Mountain Colors, Gray Mountain Scene with Snow" and you will discover the full set of mixtures for this painting. Follow the steps below to re-create it yourself.

Step 1. Begin by painting the sky blue using recipe #106. Then paint the pink horizon using recipe #64 and blend it into the previous mixture. Next, paint the distant mountain with recipe #106 and blend #108 at the base for haze. Next, paint the main mountain shape using #101. To create a haze at the bottom of the main mountain, blend #107 into the base.

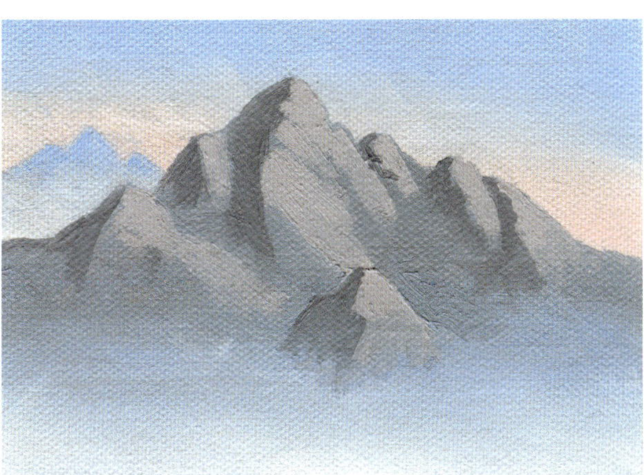

Step 2. Paint in the mountain forms using recipes #102 for the lighter side and #103 for the shadow side. This step is very important since you create the basic forms and depth of the entire mountain. Notice how a smaller peak has been developed in front of the mountain using these mixes.

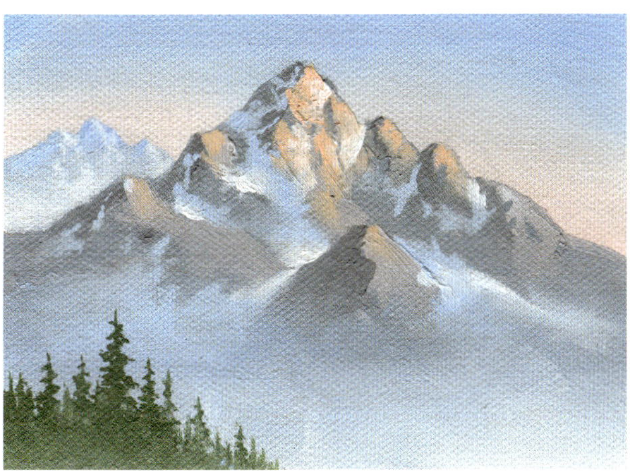

Step 3. Next, begin painting the warm, peach sunlit snow on the right sides of the mountain using recipe #105. Then use #106 for the blue shadowed snow. Add the highlights using recipe #108. Use a mix of #107 and #108 to enhance the base haze. Finally, paint the distant pine trees using #104.

LandscapeColorRecipes

COLORS USED

- Cadmium Vermilion
- Cadmium Red Light
- Zinc Yellow Hue
- Yellow Ochre
- Venetian Red
- Ivory Black
- Burnt Umber
- Raw Sienna
- Alizarin Crimson
- Cadmium Orange
- Cerulean Blue Hue
- Thalo® Blue
- Permanent Blue
- Cadmium Yellow Light
- Titanium White

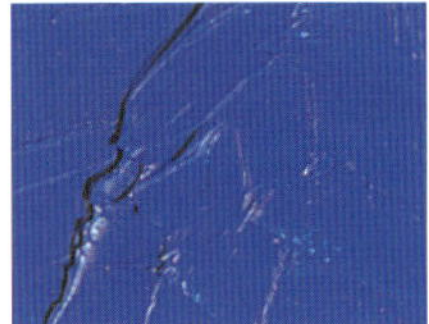

1. 1 white
4 permanent blue

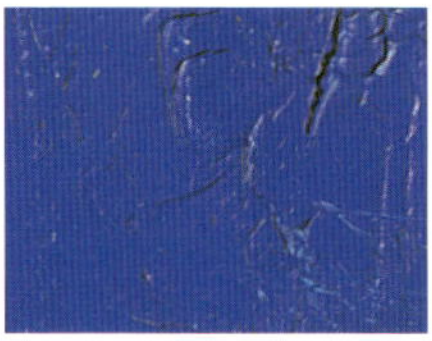

2. 2 permanent blue
1 white
1 • alizarin crimson

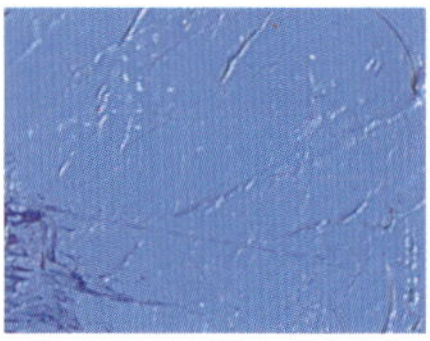

3. 2 white
1 permanent blue
1 • cerulean blue hue

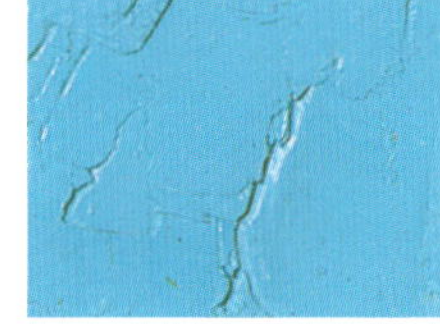

4. 1 white
1 • Thalo® blue

5. 2 white
1 zinc yellow hue
1 • cadmium orange

6. 1 white
1 • yellow ochre

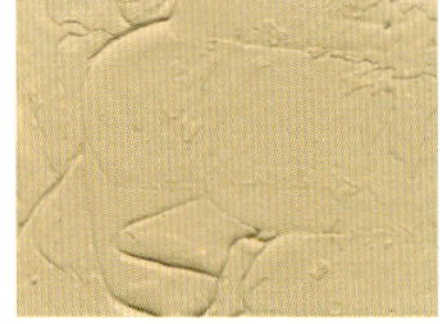

7. 8 white
1 yellow ochre
1 • permanent blue

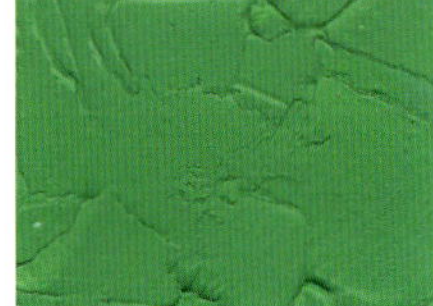

8. 6 white
1 Thalo® blue
4 zinc yellow hue

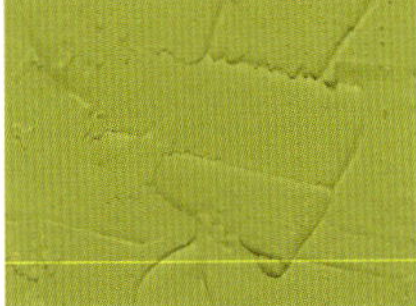

9. 7 white
1 ivory black
3 cadmium yellow light

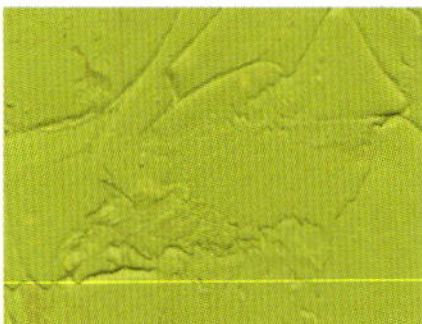

10. 4 zinc yellow hue
1 • cerulean blue hue
1 • raw sienna

11. 8 cadmium yellow light
1 cerulean blue hue

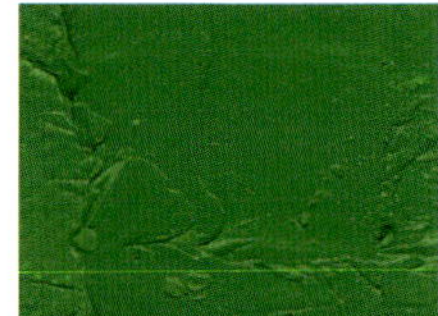

12. 5 zinc yellow hue
1 Thalo® blue

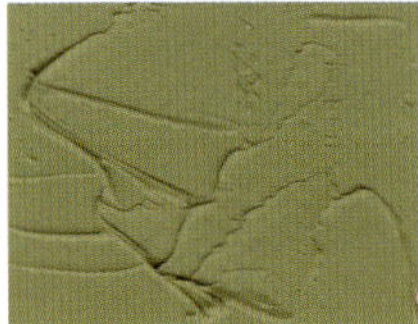

13. 5 white
3 yellow ochre
1 permanent blue

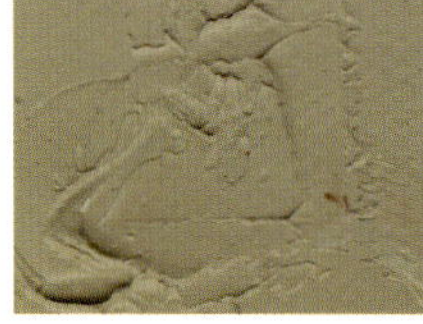

14. 5 white
1 • burnt umber

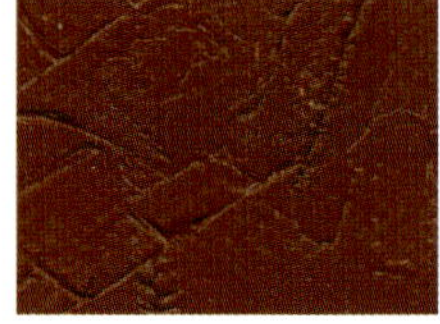

15. 2 cadmium vermilion
1 ivory black

16. 8 cadmium vermilion
1 ivory black

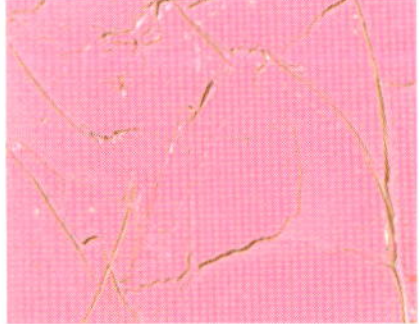

17. 5 white
1 • alizarin crimson

18. 4 white
1 cadmium red light
7 zinc yellow hue

19. 3 white
1 Venetian red

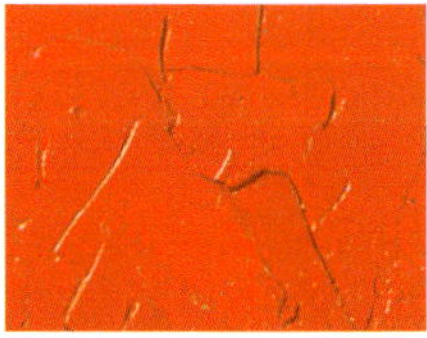

20. cadmium vermilion

LandscapeColorRecipes

COLORS USED

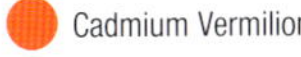

- Cadmium Vermilion
- Cadmium Orange
- Permanent Green Light
- Raw Sienna
- Ivory Black
- Yellow Ochre
- Zinc Yellow Hue
- Burnt Sienna
- Titanium White
- Cobalt Violet
- Cadmium Yellow Light
- Permanent Blue

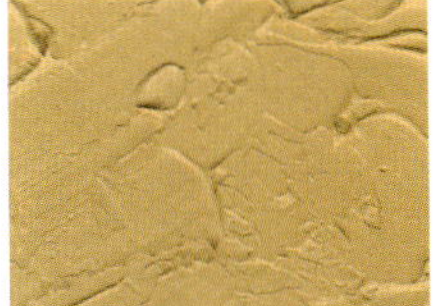

21. 3 white
1 raw sienna
1 • zinc yellow hue

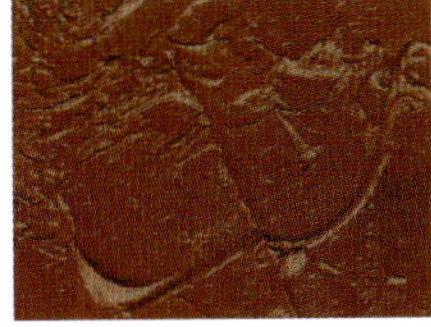

22. 2 cadmium vermilion
1 ivory black

23. 1 cobalt violet
1 cadmium orange
1 zinc yellow hue

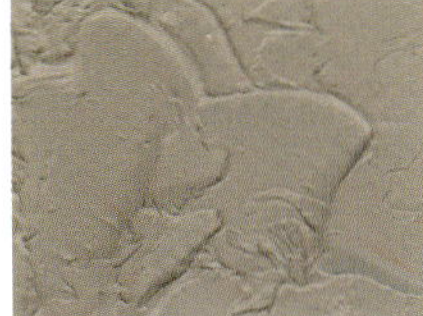

24. 7 white
1 ivory black
1 • cadmium vermilion

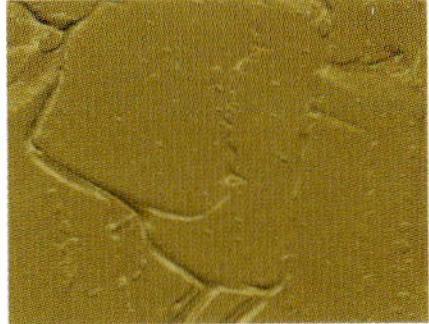

25. 1 cadmium yellow light
1 cobalt violet

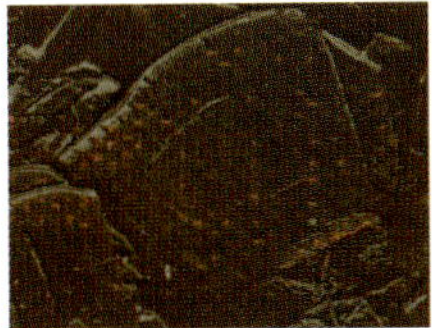

26. 1 burnt sienna
2 permanent green light

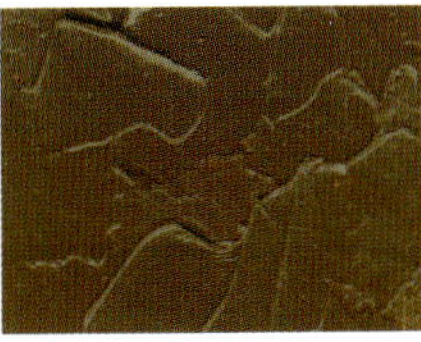

27. 3 permanent green light
1 cadmium vermilion

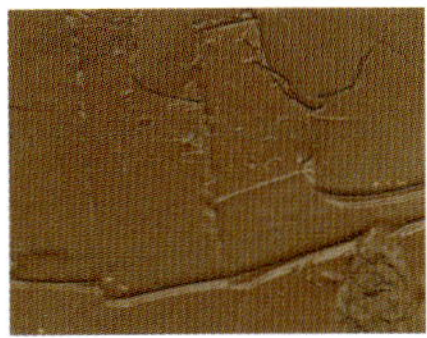

28. 1 cadmium vermilion
1 ivory black
4 raw sienna
1 white

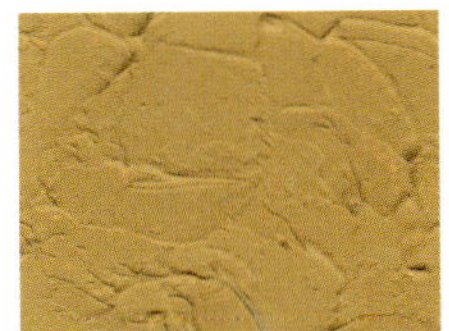

29. 1 white
2 yellow ochre

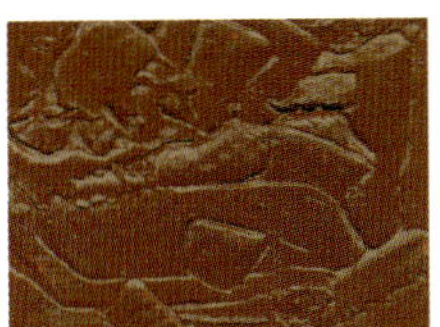

30. 1 burnt sienna
1 raw sienna

31. 3 raw sienna
1 white

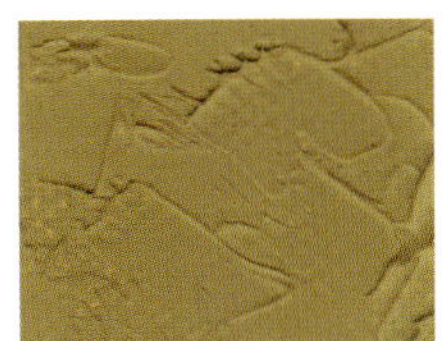

32. 2 white
2 cadmium orange
1 permanent green light

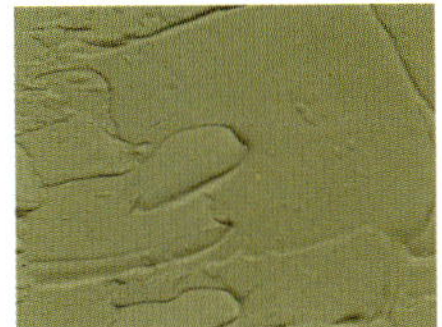

33. 5 white
3 yellow ochre
1 permanent blue

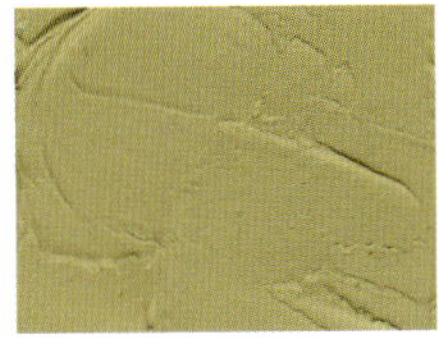

34. 5 white
2 yellow ochre
3 • permanent blue

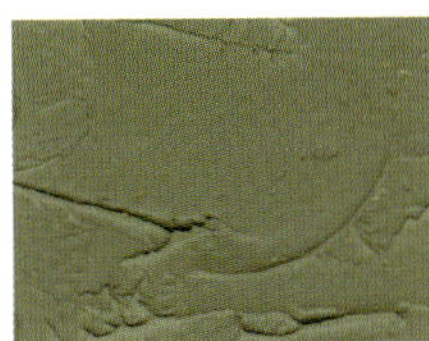

35. 3 white
2 raw sienna
1 ultramarine blue
1 • burnt sienna

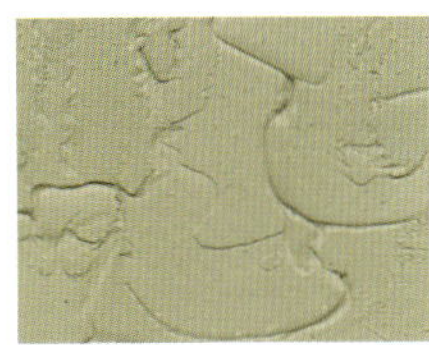

36. 3 white
1 #35
1 • raw sienna

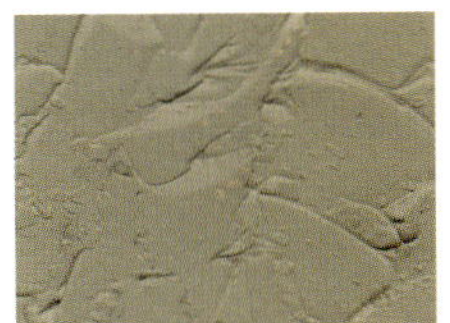

37. 5 white
1 burnt sienna
1 permanent blue

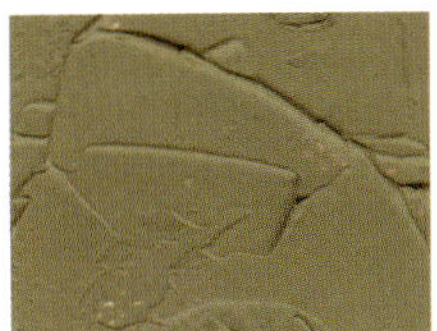

38. 8 white
2 burnt sienna
1 permanent blue

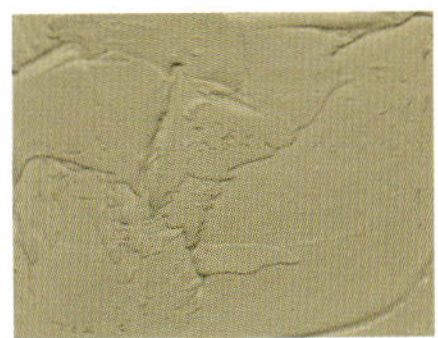

39. 2 white
1 #38

40. 3 white
1 yellow ochre

Landscape Color Recipes

COLORS USED

- Cobalt Violet Hue
- Cadmium Vermilion
- Cadmium Orange
- Cadmium Yellow Medium
- Zinc Yellow Hue
- Naples Yellow Hue
- Permanent Blue
- Cadmium Yellow Light
- Ivory Black
- Burnt Sienna
- Cerulean Blue Hue
- Titanium White
- Burnt Umber
- Cadmium Red Light
- Yellow Ochre

41. 2 raw sienna
1 cobalt violet
1 • cadmium vermilion

42. 1 ivory black
1 • permanent blue

43. 1 burnt umber
1 • cadmium vermilion

44. 2 raw sienna
1 permanent green light

45. 3 Naples yellow hue
2 burnt sienna
1 • cadmium vermilion

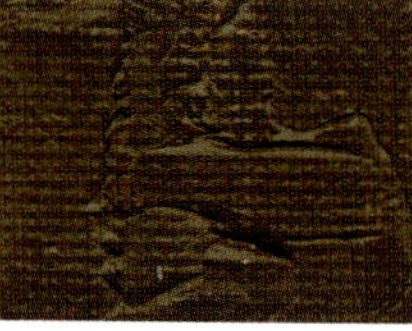

46. 1 cadmium yellow medium
1 burnt umber
1 • cadmium orange

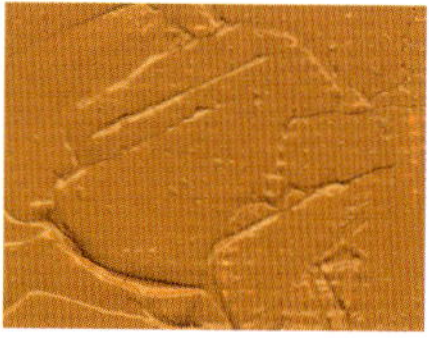

47. 1 cadmium yellow medium
1 cobalt violet
1 • burnt sienna

48. 4 white
1 burnt sienna
2 • burnt umber

49. 3 white
1 burnt umber
2 • burnt sienna

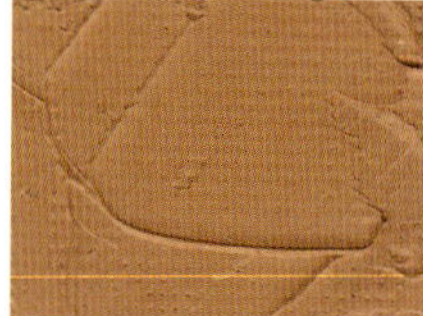

50. 6 white
1 burnt sienna
2 raw sienna

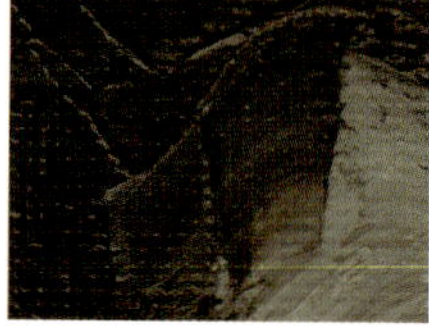

51. 1 burnt umber
1 permanent blue
1 • Naples yellow hue

52. 1 white
1 burnt umber
1 • burnt sienna

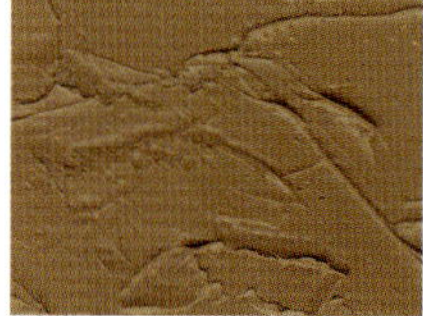

53. 2 white
1 burnt sienna
1 raw sienna
2 • permanent blue

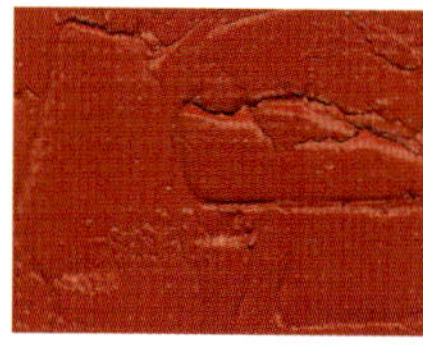

54. 1 cadmium vermilion
2 • ivory black

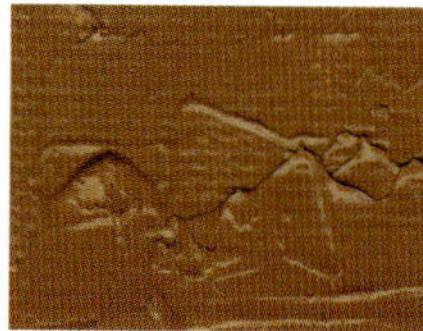

55. 4 cadmium orange
1 cerulean blue hue

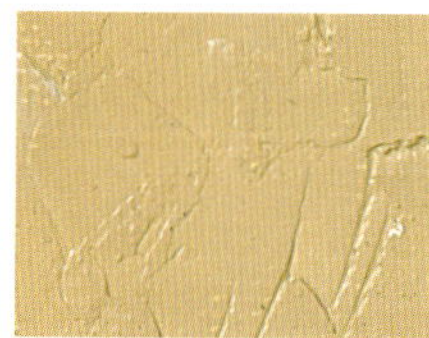

56. 8 white
1 yellow ochre
1 • permanent blue

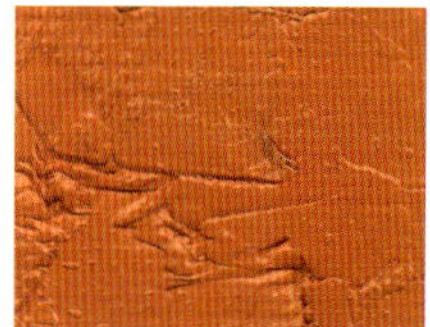

57. 2 cadmium yellow medium
1 cadmium vermilion
1 • burnt umber

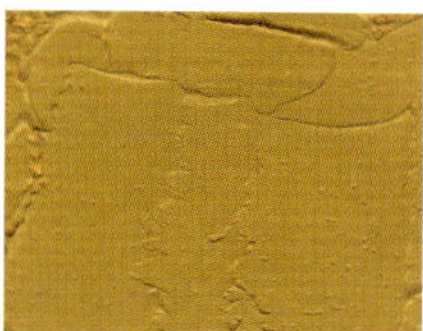

58. 2 cadmium yellow light
1 cobalt violet hue

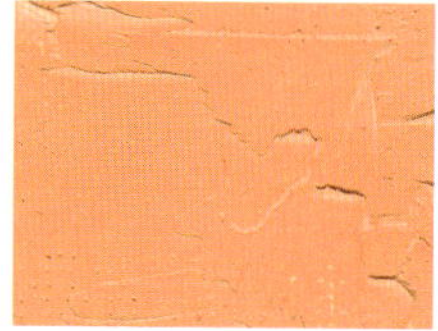

59. 6 white
7 Naples yellow hue
1 cadmium red light

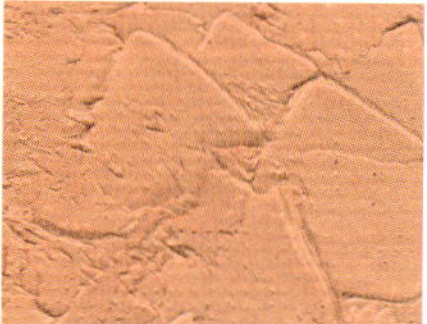

60. 3 white
1 burnt sienna

LandscapeColorRecipes

COLORS USED

- Titanium White
- Alizarin Crimson
- Ivory Black
- Cerulean Blue Hue
- Naples Yellow Hue
- Cadmium Orange
- Cobalt Blue
- Cadmium Red Light
- Zinc Yellow Hue
- Cobalt Violet
- Ultramarine Blue
- Venetian Red

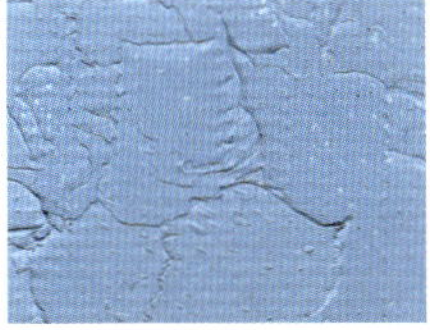

61. 6 white
1 cerulean blue hue
1 cobalt blue
1 cobalt violet hue

62. 8 white
1 cerulean blue hue

63. 3 white
2 • alizarin crimson
1 • zinc yellow hue

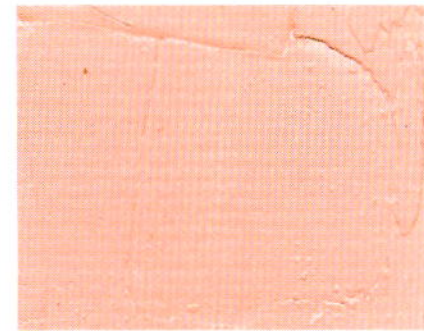

64. 3 white
1 • cadmium red light

65. 2 white
3 • Naples yellow hue

66. 2 white
1 cobalt blue
1 • cadmium red light

67. 2 white
2 • cobalt blue
1 • cadmium red light

68. 5 white
3 • cerulean blue hue
1 • cadmium red light
1 • cadmium orange

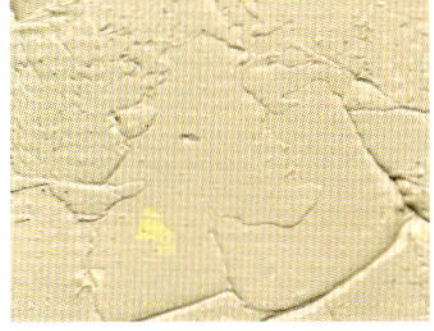

69. 2 white
1 • cadmium orange
1 • cerulean blue hue

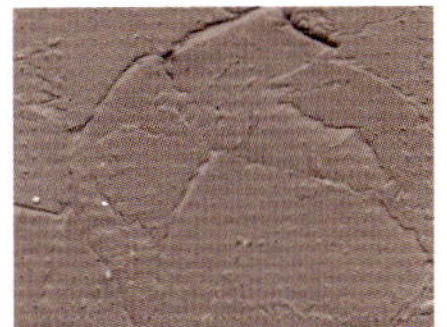

70. 7 white
1 permanent blue
2 • Venetian red

71. 2 white
1 • cadmium orange
1 • cobalt blue

72. 2 white
2 • ivory black
1 • cadmium red light

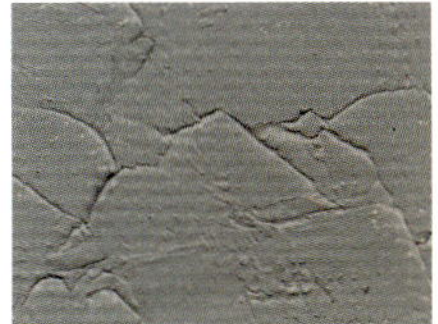

73. 1 #72
1 • cobalt blue
1 • ivory black

74. 2 white
1 • cadmium orange

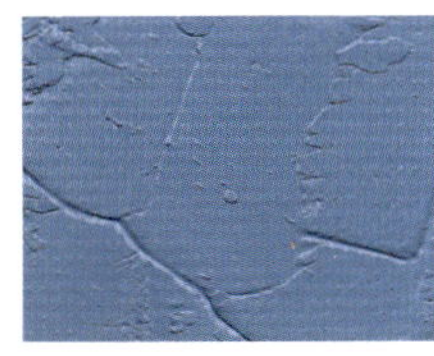

75. 3 white
4 • ivory black
3 • cobalt violet hue

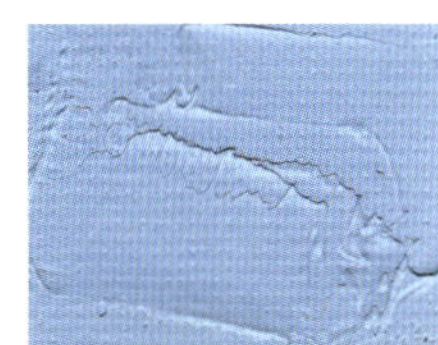

76. 4 white
1 cobalt blue
3 • cobalt violet hue

77. 6 white
1 • cadmium orange
1 • alizarin crimson

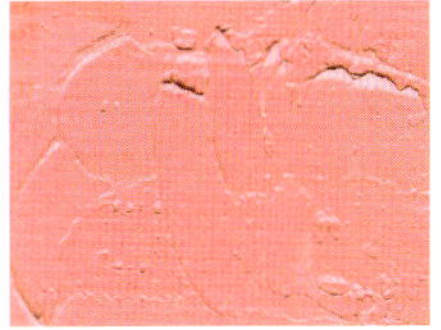

78. 2 white
1 • alizarin crimson
1 • cadmium orange

79. 4 white
1 • cadmium orange

80. 1 #75
1 • ivory black
1 • alizarin crimson

LandscapeColorRecipes

COLORS USED

- Titanium White
- Yellow Ochre
- Cadmium Orange
- Ivory Black
- Burnt Umber
- Naples Yellow Hue
- Cadmium Red Light
- Raw Sienna
- Thalo® Blue
- Cadmium Yellow Medium
- Zinc Yellow Hue
- Permanent Green Light
- Permanent Blue
- Cadmium Yellow Light
- Cerulean Blue Hue

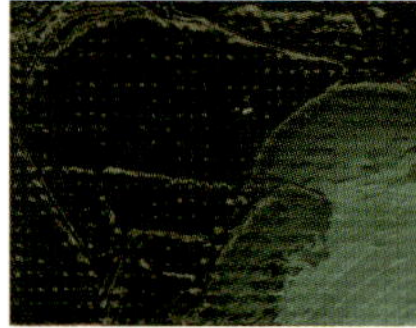

81. 2 burnt umber
1 Thalo® blue

82. 3 yellow ochre
1 permanent blue

83. 1 cadmium yellow medium
3 • permanent blue

84. 1 cadmium yellow light
2 • permanent blue

85. 2 zinc yellow hue
1 • cerulean blue hue

86. 1 zinc yellow hue
2 • #85
2 • white

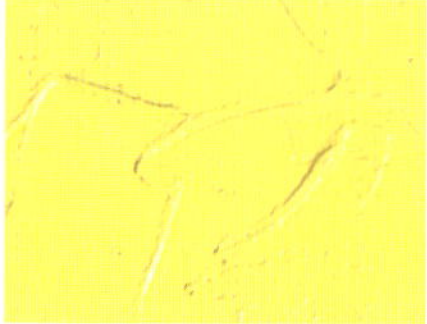

87. 1 #86
1 white

88. 2 cerulean blue hue
2 Naples yellow hue
1 cadmium orange

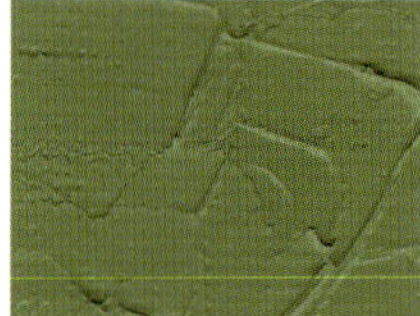

89. 1 #88
1 #90
1 • cerulean blue hue

90. 1 #88
1 white
1 • cadmium yellow light

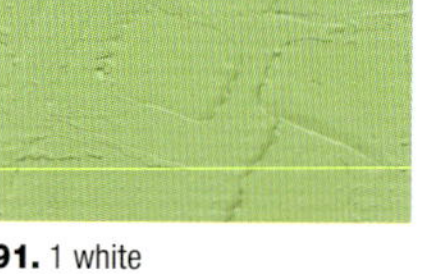

91. 1 white
3 • cadmium yellow light
1 • ivory black
1 • cerulean blue hue

92. 3 cerulean blue
1 raw sienna
1 • Naples yellow hue

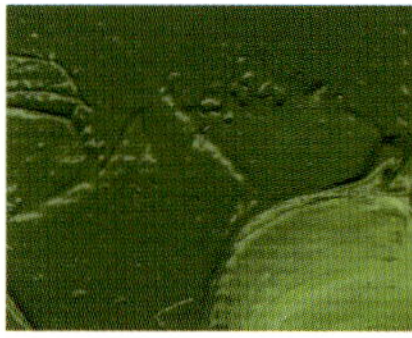

93. 1 permanent green light
2 • cadmium red light

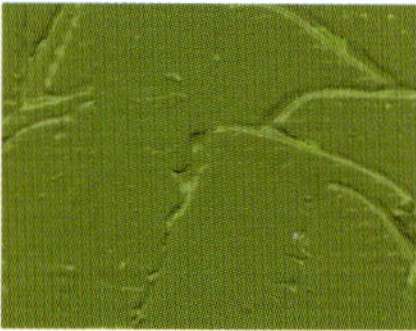

94. 3 cadmium yellow medium
1 • Thalo® blue

95. 3 cadmium yellow light
1 permanent green light
3 • white

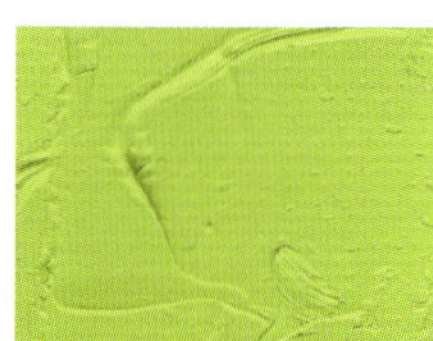

96. 1 #95
1 white

97. 3 cerulean blue
1 Naples yellow hue
1 cadmium orange

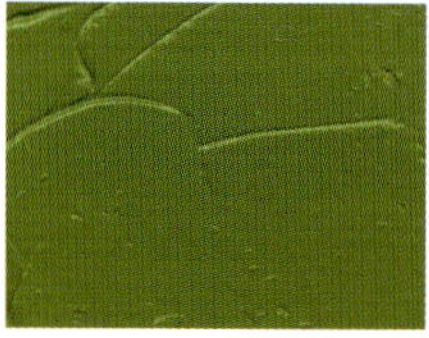

98. 1 cadmium yellow medium
1 • Thalo® blue
1 • cadmium red light

99. 1 #98
2 cadmium yellow light
1 • cadmium orange

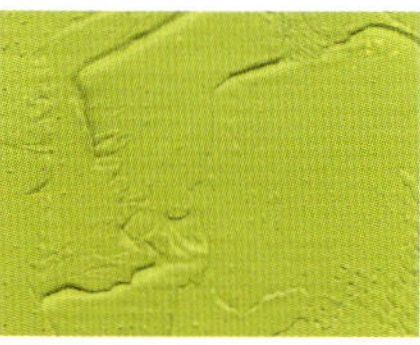

100. 2 zinc yellow hue
2 • permanent green light
2 • cadmium orange
1 white

COLORS USED

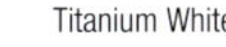

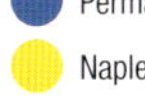
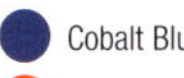
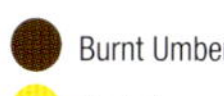

- Titanium White
- Alizarin Crimson
- Ivory Black
- Yellow Ochre
- Permanent Blue
- Naples Yellow Hue
- Cadmium Orange
- Burnt Sienna
- Cobalt Blue
- Cadmium Red Light
- Zinc Yellow Hue
- Raw Sienna
- Cadmium Vermilion
- Cerulean Blue Hue
- Cadmium Yellow Medium
- Burnt Umber
- Cadmium Yellow Light

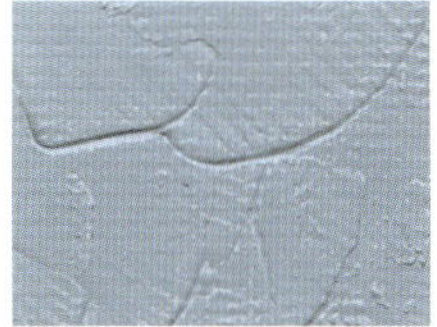

101. 5 white
1 permanent blue
1 • cadmium red light

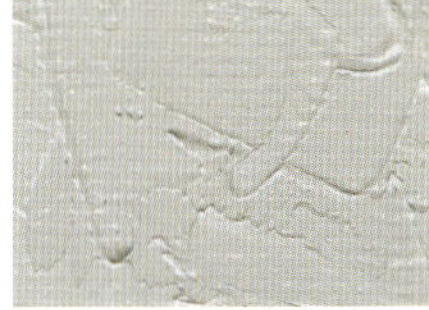

102. 3 white
1 • cadmium red light
4 • permanent blue

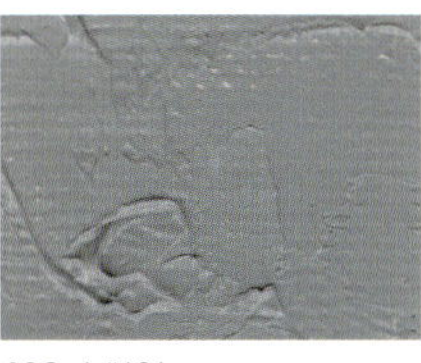

103. 1 #101
1 permanent blue
2 • cadmium red light

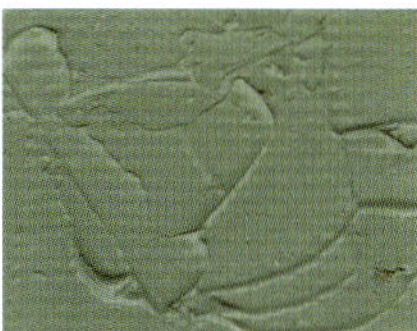

104. 2 white
2 permanent blue
1 yellow ochre

105. 2.5 white
1 • cadmium orange

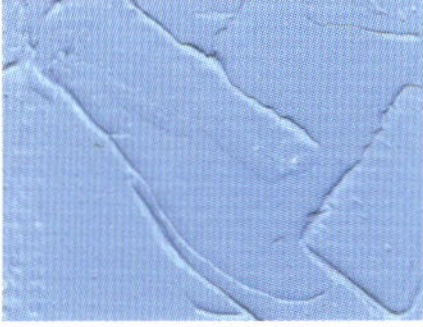

106. 10 white
1 permanent blue

107. 2 white
3 • permanent blue

108. 6 white
1 • Naples yellow hue

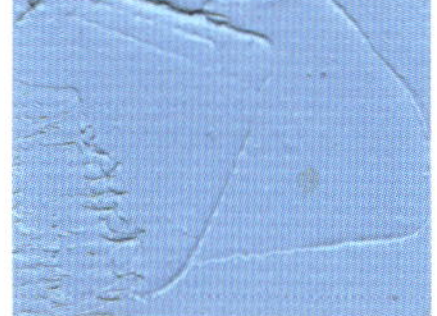

109. 4 white
1 cobalt blue

110. 2 white
4 • cerulean blue hue

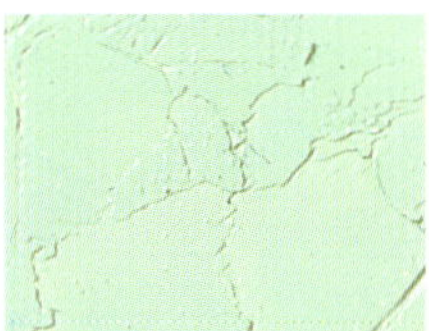

111. 2 white
1 • cerulean blue hue
1 • Naples yellow hue

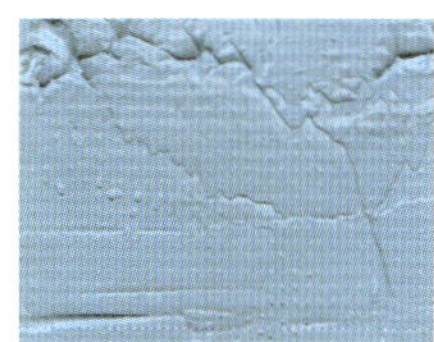

112. 2 #109
1 • ivory black

113. 3 white
2 • zinc yellow hue

114. 7 white
1 cerulean blue hue

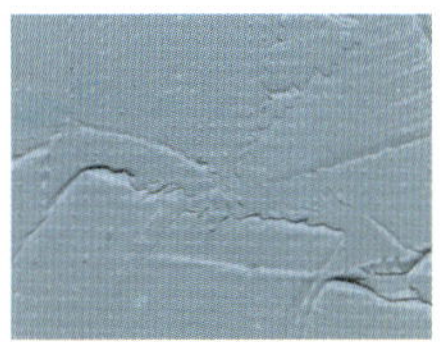

115. 3 white
2 cobalt blue
3 • ivory black

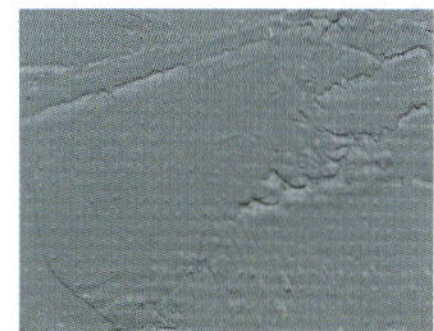

116. 1 #115
3 • cobalt blue
2 • ivory black

117. 2 white
1 • cadmium orange

118. 1 white
1 • cadmium yellow light

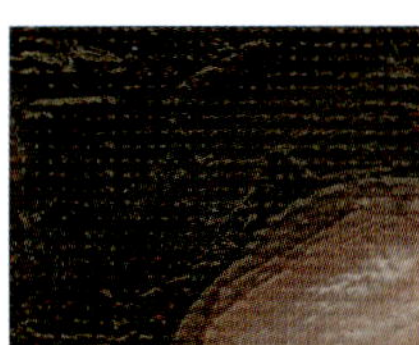

119. 1 burnt umber
1 alizarin crimson

120. 1 white
2 • #119
2 • permanent blue

LandscapeColorRecipes

COLORS USED

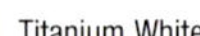

Titanium White	Burnt Umber	Cobalt Blue	Permanent Blue
Raw Umber	Naples Yellow Hue	Cadmium Yellow Medium	Cadmium Yellow Light
Cadmium Orange	Cadmium Red Light	Zinc Yellow Hue	Cerulean Blue Hue
Ivory Black	Raw Sienna	Venetian Red	Alizarin Crimson

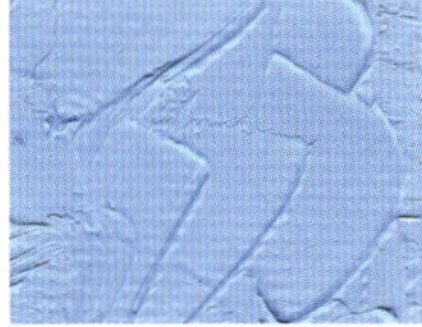

121. 2 white
1 • permanent blue

122. 1 white
1 #121

123. 4 white
1 permanent blue
2 • cerulean blue hue

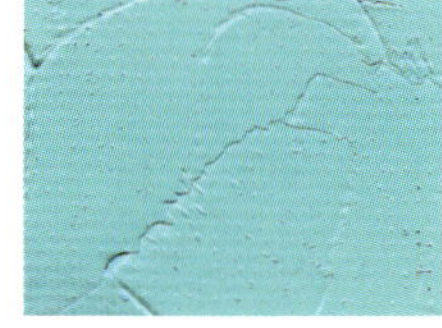

124. 2 white
1 cerulean blue hue

125. 3 white
3 cobalt blue
3 • ivory black

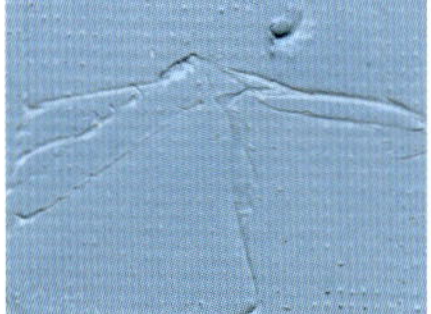

126. 1 #125
1 white
1 • cerulean blue hue

127. 3 white
3 • cerulean blue hue
2 • cobalt blue

128. 3 white
2 • cobalt blue
2 • ivory black
1 • raw umber

129. 4 white
2 • Naples yellow hue
1 • cadmium orange

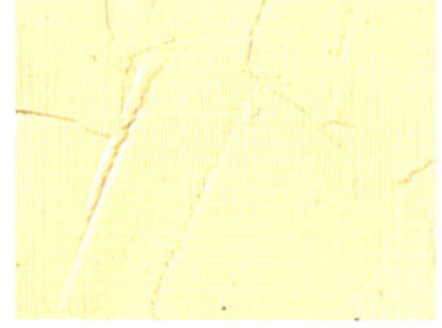

130. 3 white
2 • Naples yellow hue

131. 1.5 white
1 • cadmium yellow light
1 • zinc yellow hue

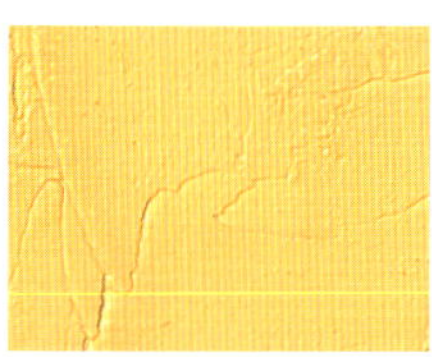

132. 2 white
2 • cadmium yellow med

133. 2 #132
1 • cadmium red light

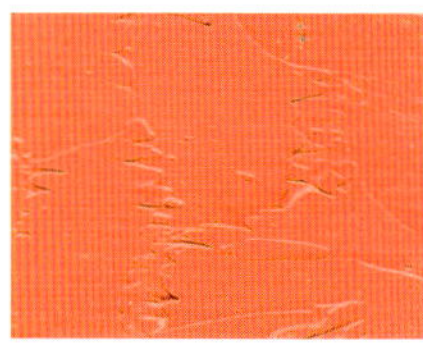

134. 2 white
3 • cadmium red light
2 • cadmium orange

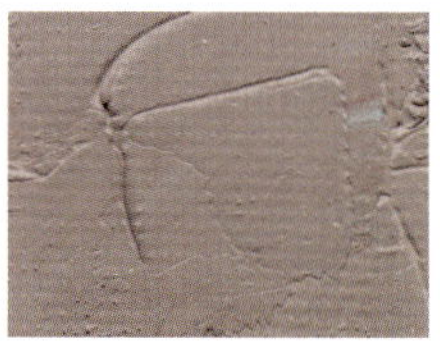

135. 2 white
4 • cobalt blue
1 • Venetian red

136. 2 white
2 • cerulean blue hue
1 • #133
1 • raw sienna

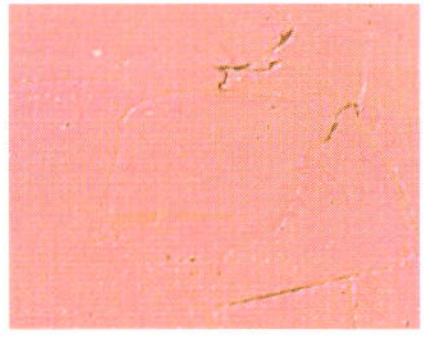

137. 4 white
3 • alizarin crimson

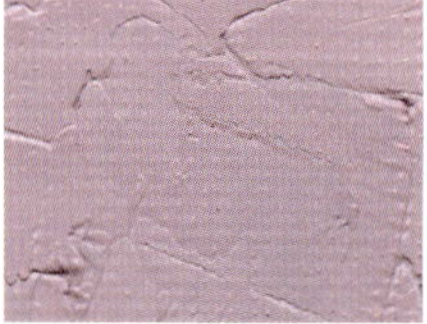

138. 1 #137
1 • permanent blue

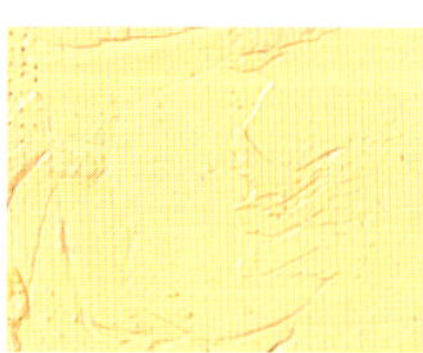

139. 1 white
1 • cadmium yellow light
1 • #137

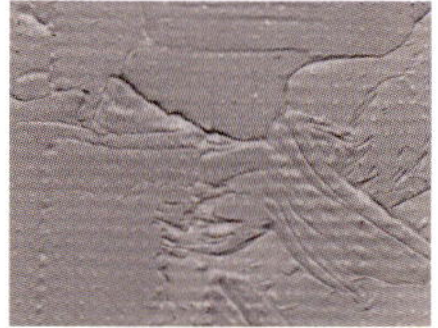

140. 1 #137
2 • permanent blue
1 • burnt umber

LandscapeColorRecipes

COLORS USED

- Titanium White
- Alizarin Crimson
- Ivory Black
- Permanent Blue
- Naples Yellow Hue
- Cadmium Orange
- Cobalt Blue
- Cadmium Yellow Light
- Thalo® Blue
- Cadmium Red Light
- Raw Umber
- Burnt Umber

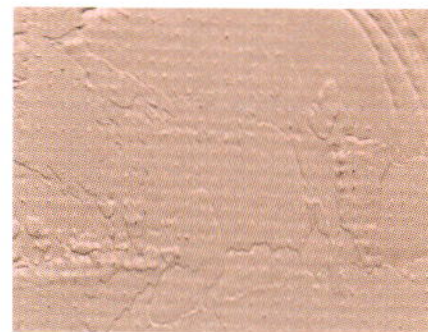

141. 1 white
1 • burnt umber
1 • alizarin crimson

142. 2 white
1 Naples yellow hue
1 • alizarin crimson
1 • cadmium yellow light

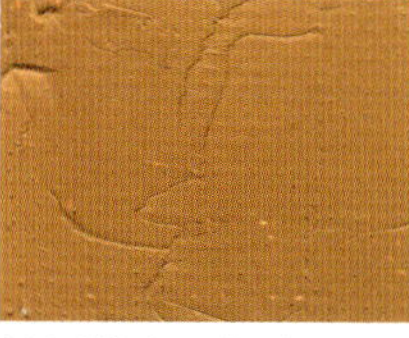

143. 2 Naples yellow hue
2 • allizarin crimson
1 • burnt umber

144. 1 #143
1 • alizarin crimson
1 • permanent blue

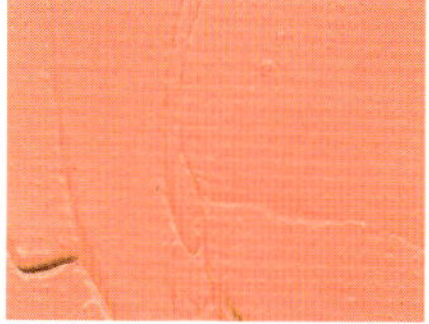

145. 3 white
4 • cadmium orange
1 • alizarin crimson
2 • cadmium red light

146. 2 #145
1 • permanent blue

147. 3 white
1 permanent blue
3 • alizarin crimson
1 • raw umber

148. 2 white
1 Naples yellow hue

149. 2 white
2 • Thalo® blue
1 • ivory black

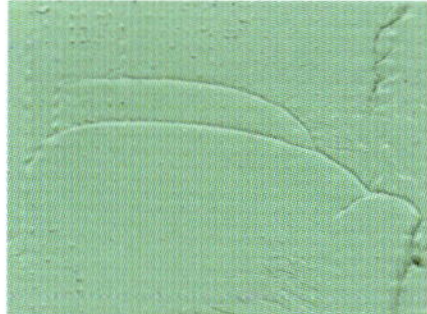

150. 1 #148
1 #149

151. 10 white
1 Thalo® blue
2 ivory black

152. 1 #151
3 • ivory black

153. 3 #148
1 #149

154. 2 white
1 • raw umber
1 • cobalt blue

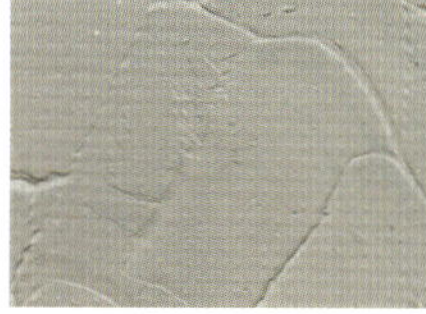

155. 2 white
2 • raw umber
1 • cobalt blue

156. 2 white
4 • burnt umber
4 • permanent blue

157. 4 white
1 • cadmium orange
1 • cobalt blue

158. 2 white
1 #157

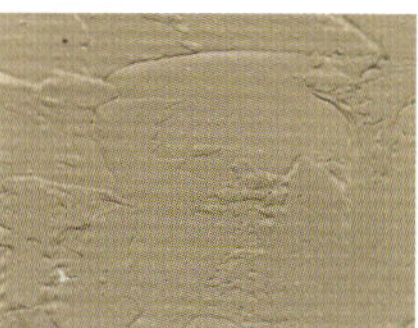

159. 10 white
1 burnt umber

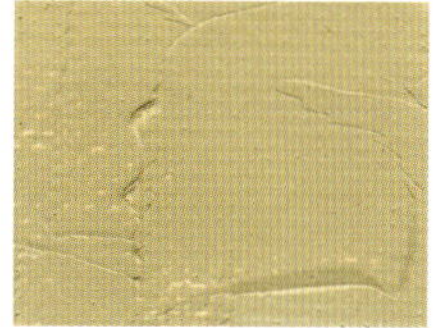

160. 8 white
1 yellow ochre
2 • permanent blue

LandscapeColorRecipes

COLORS USED

- Titanium White
- Yellow Ochre
- Cobalt Blue
- Ivory Black
- Burnt Umber
- Naples Yellow Hue
- Raw Umber
- Raw Sienna
- Thalo® Blue
- Alizarin Crimson
- Cadmium Yellow Medium
- Permanent Green Light
- Permanent Blue
- Cadmium Yellow Light
- Cerulean Blue Hue
- Burnt Sienna

161. 8 cadmium yellow medium
1 Thalo® blue
2 • alizarin crimson

162. 2 Naples yellow hue
1 #161

163. 1 #162
4 • cadmium yellow light
4 • white

164. 2 white
2 • raw umber

165. 8 white
1 • yellow ochre
1 • cerulean blue hue

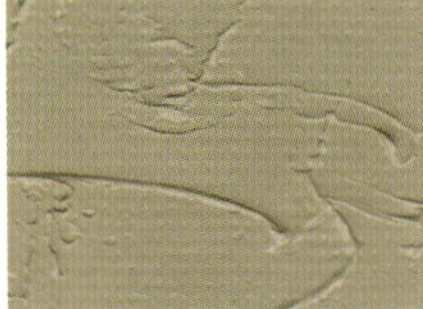

166. 2 white
3 • burnt umber

167. 1 white
1 raw umber
2 • ivory black

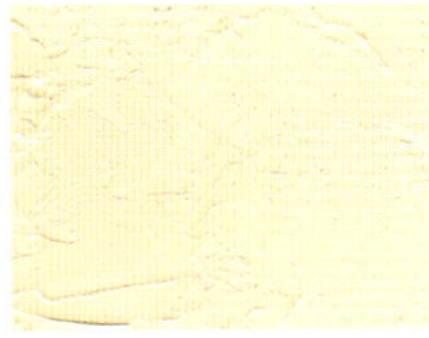

168. 8 white
1 • yellow ochre

169. 2 permanent green light
1 yellow ochre
2 • permanent blue

170. 1 Naples yellow hue
1 permanent green light

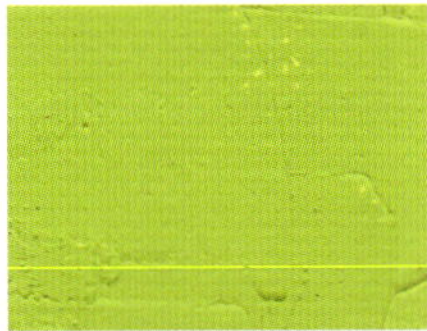

171. 1 white
1 cadmium yellow light
3 • permanent green light

172. 2 white
4 burnt umber
3 • cobalt blue

173. 1 cobalt blue
2 Naples yellow hue

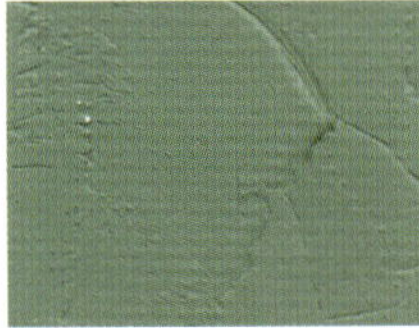

174. 2 cobalt blue
1 Naples yellow hue
1 white
3 • raw sienna

175. 1 white
2 • cobalt blue
2 • cerulean blue hue
1 • raw sienna

176. 1 raw sienna
1 cerulean blue hue
2 white

177. 2 #176
1 cerulean blue hue
3 • burnt sienna

178. 1 #176
3 • cadmium yellow light
1 white

179. 2 #176
1 cadmium yellow light
3 • Naples yellow hue

180. 2 white
2 • raw sienna
1 • cerulean blue hue
2 • Naples yellow hue

COLORS USED

Titanium White
Viridian Green
Permanent Green Light
Raw Sienna
Permanent Blue
Naples Yellow Hue
Thalo® Blue
Burnt Sienna
Cobalt Blue
Cadmium Yellow Light
Zinc Yellow Hue
Burnt Umber
Venetian Red
Cerulean Blue Hue
Cadmium Yellow Medium

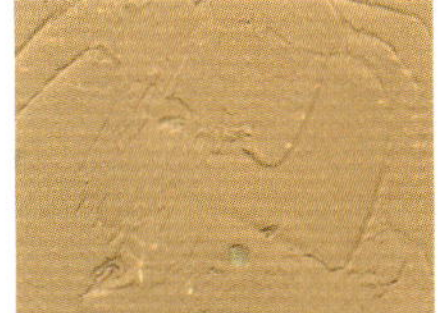

181. 2 white
1 raw sienna
1 • burnt sienna

182. 2 #181
1 burnt umber
2 burnt sienna

183. 6 burnt umber
1 Venetian red
4 • permanent blue

184. 3 white
3 • viridian green
1 • #188

185. 2 permanent blue
2 cadmium yellow medium
3 • cadmium yellow light

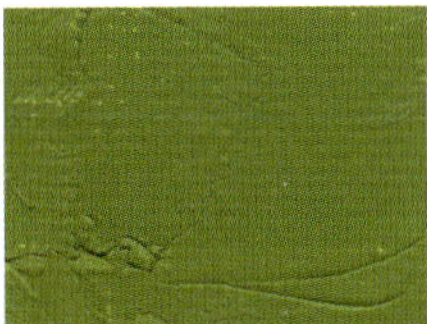

186. 2 permanent blue
1 cadmium yellow light
2 Naples yellow hue
1 cadmium yellow medium

187. 1 #186
3 • cadmium yellow light
2 • white

188. 2 cerulean blue hue
1 cadmium yellow light
2 • white
1 • burnt sienna

189. 1 #188
2 Naples yellow hue

190. 1 zinc yellow hue
2 • #189
2 white
2 • cobalt blue

191. 2 permanent blue
2 cadmium yellow medium
3 • Thalo® blue
3 • burnt sienna

192. 2 #191
1 cadmium yellow medium

193. 2 #192
1 cadmium yellow light
1 • white

194. 1 permanent green light
2 • cadmium yellow med.

195. 1 #194
2 #196

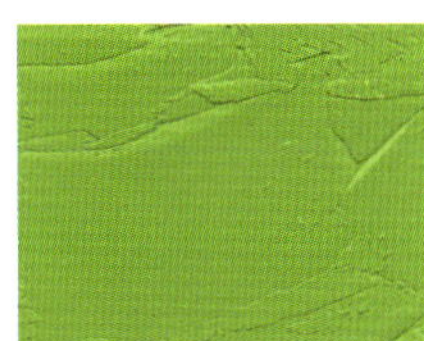

196. 1 permanent green light
2 cadmium yellow light
1 • white

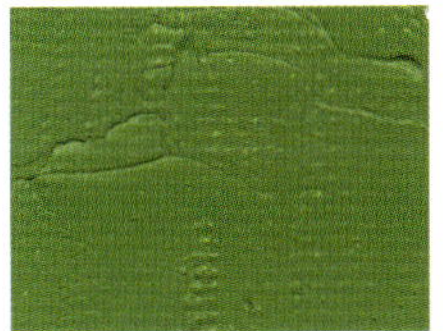

197. 1.5 cadmium yellow light
2 permanent blue

198. 1 #197
1 #199

199. 1 #197
1 cadmium yellow light
1 • white

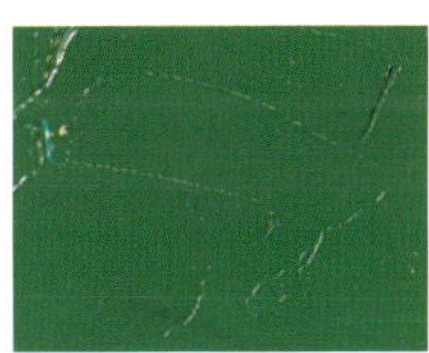

200. 1 cadmium yellow medium
1 Thalo® blue
1 white

LandscapeColorRecipes

COLORS USED

Titanium White
Yellow Ochre
Burnt Sienna
Ivory Black
Burnt Umber
Naples Yellow Hue
Raw Umber
Cobalt Blue
Viridian Green
Cadmium Yellow Medium
Cobalt Violet Hue
Permanent Green Light
Permanent Blue
Cadmium Yellow Light
Cerulean Blue Hue

201. 2 white
1 permanent green light

202. 3 viridian green
4 white
1 cadmium yellow medium

203. 2 permanent blue
1 cadmium yellow light
2 Naples yellow hue
1 cadmium yellow medium

204. 1 #203
1 Naples yellow hue

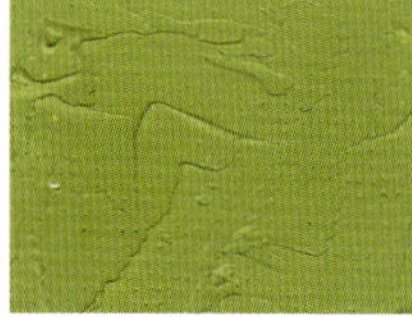

205. 1 #204
1 Naples yellow hue
2 • white

206. 2 white
2 • raw umber
1 • burnt umber

207. 3 white
1 raw umber

208. 2 white
1 • burnt umber

209. 3 white
1 • ivory black

210. 3 white
3 • ivory black
1 • raw umber

211. 8 white
1 ivory black
1 • cerulean blue hue

212. 5 white
1 • yellow ochre

213. 1 white
4 • cobalt violet hue
2 • burnt umber
1 • cobalt blue

214. 1 burnt umber
1 cobalt blue
2 white
1 • burnt sienna

215. 2 white
2 • #214

216. 2 white
1 burnt umber
1 permanent blue

217. 1 white
2 • burnt umber
1 • permanent blue

218. 4 white
1 #217
1 • cobalt violet hue

219. 1 white
1 burnt umber
1 burnt sienna
1 ivory black

220. 5 white
1 burnt sienna
1 burnt umber

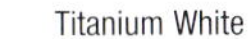

COLORS USED

- Titanium White
- Alizarin Crimson
- Ivory Black
- Yellow Ochre
- Cadmium Yellow Light
- Permanent Blue
- Naples Yellow Hue
- Raw Umber
- Burnt Sienna
- Viridian Green
- Cobalt Blue
- Permanent Green Light
- Zinc Yellow Hue
- Raw Sienna
- Thalo® Blue
- Cobalt Violet Hue
- Cadmium Yellow Medium
- Burnt Umber

221. 4 white
1 #220
2 • cobalt blue
1 • raw sienna

222. 2 ivory black
2 permanent blue
1 white

223. 1 white
4 • ivory black
1 • burnt sienna

224. 1 burnt umber
1 burnt sienna
1 white
3 • permanent blue

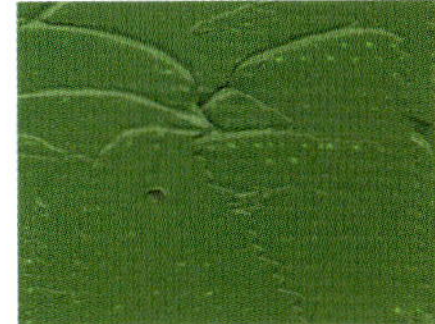

225. 2 permanent green light
2 • Thalo® blue
2 • cadmium yellow med.
2 • white

226. 2 viridian green
1 cadmium yellow light

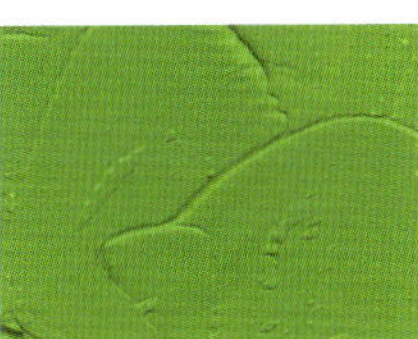

227. 1 #226
2 zinc yellow hue

228. 2 #225
1 white
1 • zinc yellow hue

229. 1 #225
1 white
1 zinc yellow hue
2 cadmium yellow light

230. 1 white
1 Naples yellow hue
1 • permanent blue

231. 2 white
5 • raw umber
5 • Naples yellow hue
1 • burnt sienna

232. 2 white
2 • zinc yellow hue
1 • raw umber

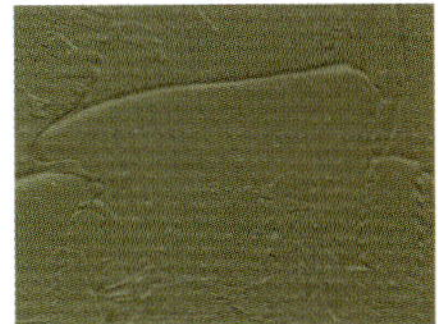

233. 2 white
1 raw umber
1 permanent green light

234. 1white
1 viridian green
1 raw sienna

235. 1 #234
3 • alizarin crimson

236. 1 white
3 • ivory black

237. 3 white
1 #136
1 • burnt sienna

238. 2 white
1 ivory black
3 • permanent blue
2 • cobalt violet hue

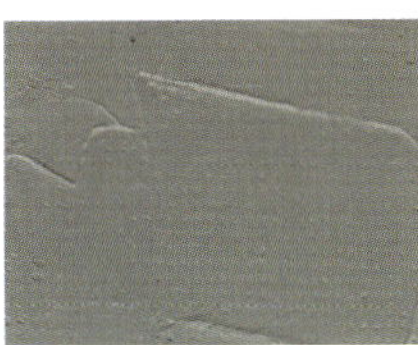

239. 3 #238
2 #237

240. 6 white
4 yellow ochre
1 permanent blue

Landscape Color Recipes

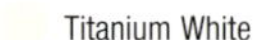

COLORS USED

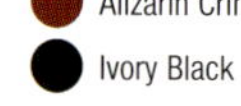

- Titanium White
- Yellow Ochre
- Cadmium Red Light
- Zinc Yellow Hue
- Burnt Umber
- Naples Yellow Hue
- Cadmium Orange
- Thalo® Red Rose
- Thalo® Blue
- Cadmium Vermilion
- Cobalt Violet Hue
- Thalo® Green (Blue Shade)
- Permanent Blue
- Cadmium Yellow Light
- Alizarin Crimson
- Ivory Black

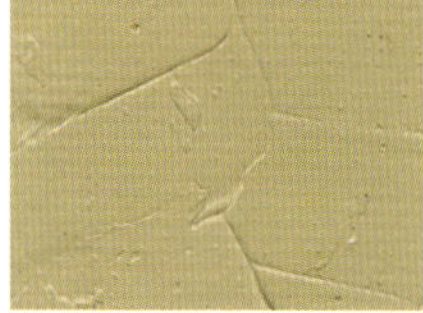

241. 2 white
3 • yellow ochre
1 • permanent blue

242. 2 burnt umber
1 Thalo® blue
4 white
2 Naples yellow hue

243. 2 burnt umber
2 Thalo® blue
5 Naples yellow hue
2 white

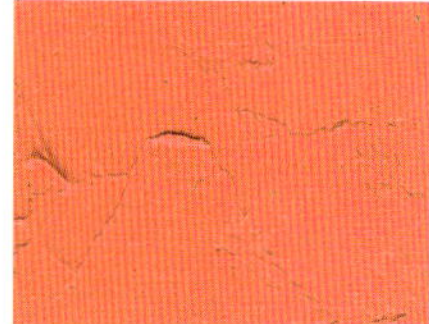

244. 4 white
1 cadmium vermilion

245. 1 yellow ochre
1 cadmium red light

246. 2 Naples yellow hue
1 cadmium yellow light
2 • cadmium orange

247. 1 white
4 alizarin crimson
2 • cadmium red light

248. 1 white
2 • cadmium vermilion

249. titanium white

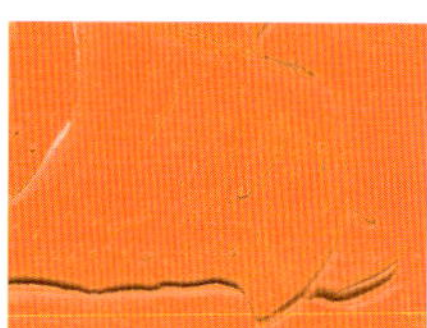

250. 6 Naples yellow hue
1 cadmium orange
1 white

251. 2 white
4 • cadmium orange

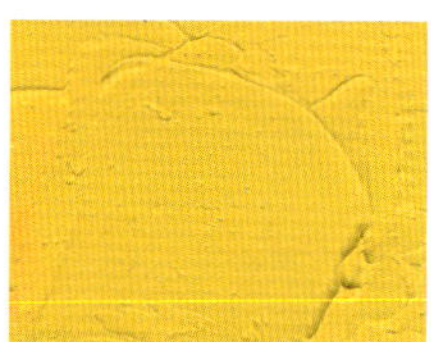

252. 3 zinc yellow hue
1 • cobalt violet hue

253. 3 white
1 Thalo® red rose

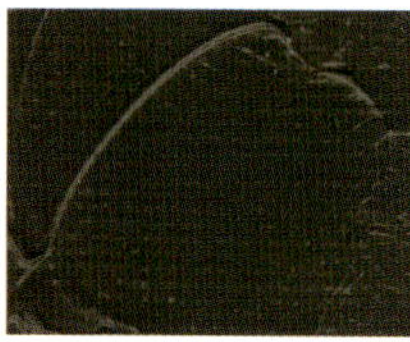

254. 3 ivory black
2 white
1 cobalt violet hue

255. 1 cadmium yellow light
3 • alizarin crimson

256. 2 zinc yellow hue
2 • cadmium orange

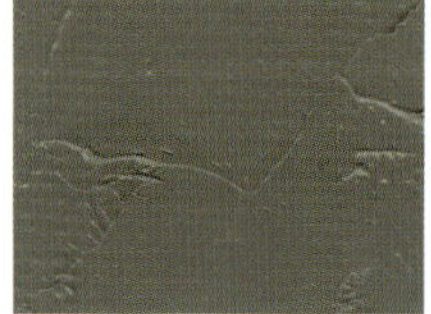

257. 2 permanent blue
1 burnt umber
4 white

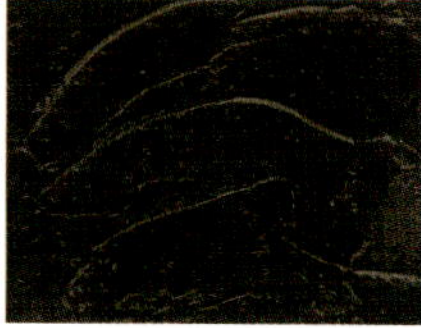

258. ivory black

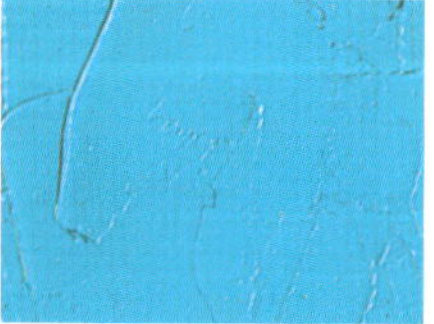

259. 1 white
2 • Thalo® blue

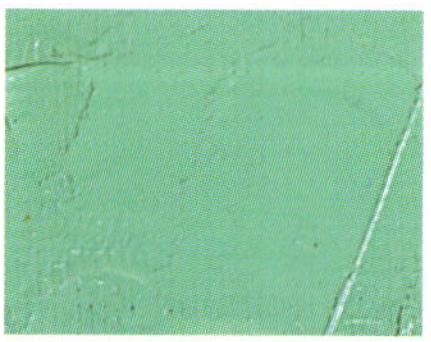

260. 2 white
2 • Thalo® green
(blue shade)

COLORS USED

- Titanium white
- Alizarin Crimson
- Ivory Black
- Burnt Umber
- Permanent Blue
- Thalo® Red Rose
- Raw Umber
- Magenta
- Cobalt Blue
- Permanent Green Light
- Cerulean Blue Hue
- Cadmium Vermilion
- Cobalt Violet Hue
- Viridian Green

261. 1 white
4 • permanent blue
1 • burnt umber
1 • alizarin crimson

262. 2 white
1 #261
1 • cerulean blue hue

263. 1 white
1 • raw umber
2 • cobalt blue

264. 1 white
2 cobalt blue
2 • cadmium vermilion

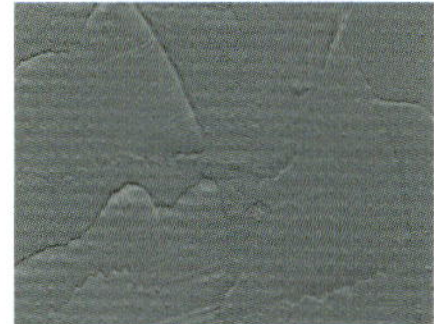

265. 1 #264
1 • ivory black

266. 1 white
2 • magenta

267. 6 cobalt violet hue
3 white
1 permanent blue

268. 2 white
1 cobalt violet hue
2 • permanent blue

269. 2 white
3 permanent blue
1 Thalo® red rose

270. 5 cobalt violet hue
1 white
2 • permanent blue

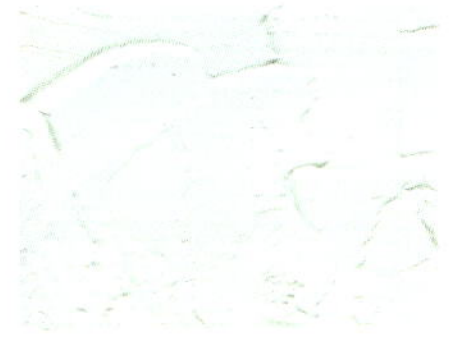

271. 3 white
1 • cerulean blue hue

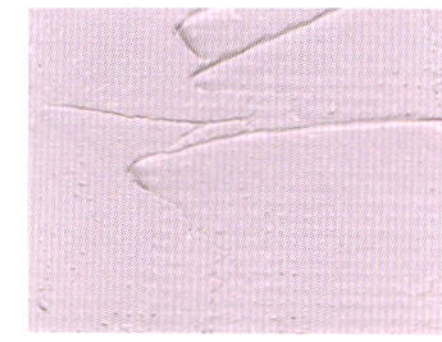

272. 8 white
1 cobalt violet hue

273. 3 cobalt violet hue
1 white
2 • burnt umber
1 • permanent blue

274. 1 #273
1 #272

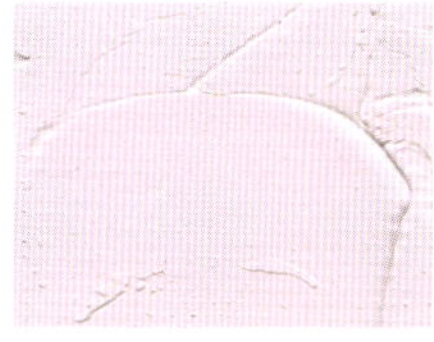

275. 1 white
2 • cobalt violet hue

276. 10 white
1 burnt umber

277. 2 white
1 burnt umber

278. 1 white
1 • viridian green
1 • raw umber

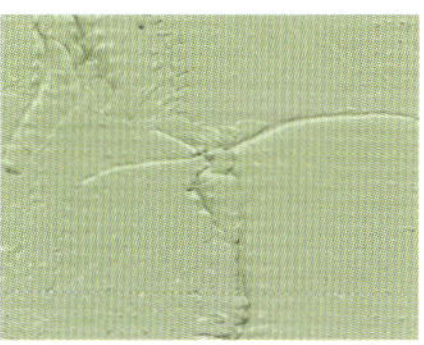

279. 1 #278
1 • permanent green light

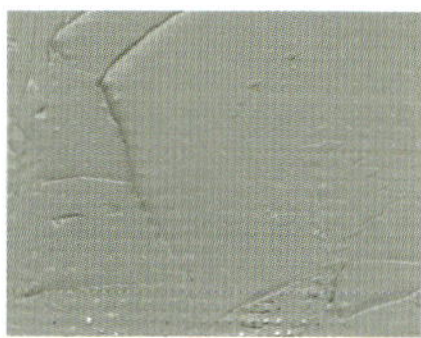

280. 1 white
1 • cerulean blue hue
3 • ivory black

LandscapeColorRecipes

COLORS USED

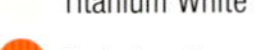
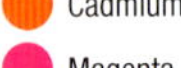

- Titanium White
- Cadmium Orange
- Magenta

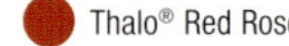

- Thalo® Red Rose
- Cadmium Red Light
- Cobalt Violet Hue

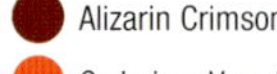

- Alizarin Crimson
- Cadmium Vermilion
- Cadmium Yellow Medium

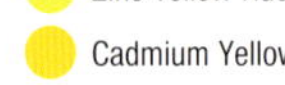

- Zinc Yellow Hue
- Cadmium Yellow Light

281. 1 white
4 • Thalo® red rose

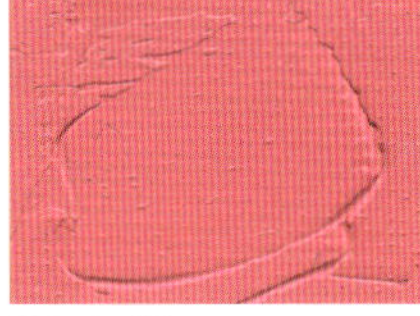

282. 1 #281
4 • alizarin crimson

283. 2 zinc yellow hue
1 cadmium orange

284. 2 white
1 cadmium red light

285. 2 cadmium yellow light
1 white

286. 2 cadmium yellow light
2 • cadmium orange
1 white

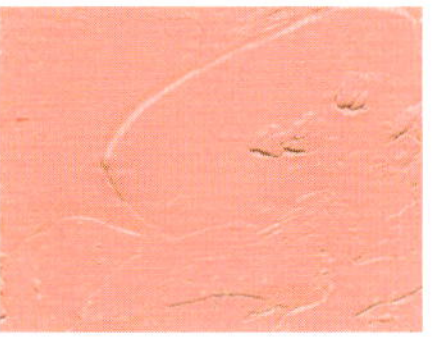

287. 1 white
1 • cadmium vermilion

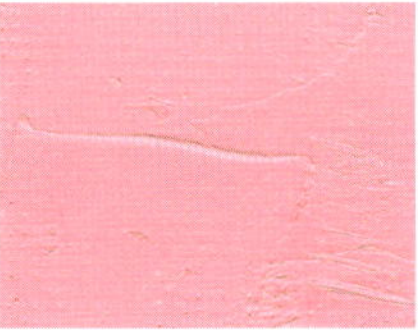

288. 1 white
2 • Thalo® red rose

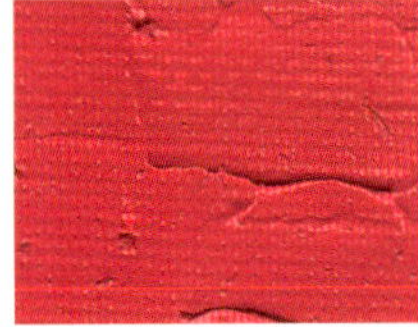

289. 4 Thalo® red rose
1 white

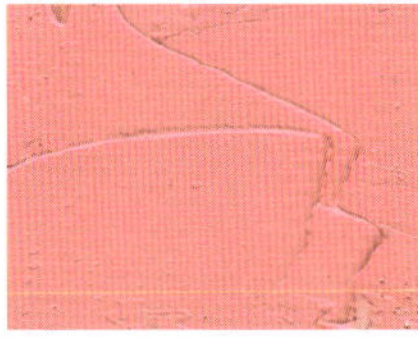

290. 1 white
3 • alizarin crimson

291. 2 magenta
1 white

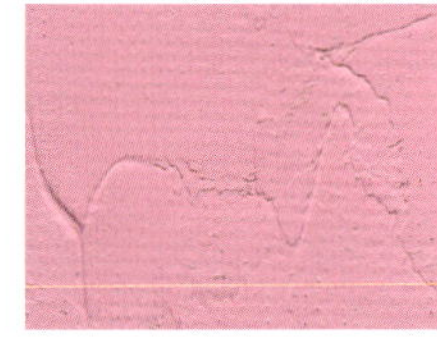

292. 1 white
2 • Thalo® red rose
2 • cobalt violet hue

293. 5 white
1.5 cadmium yellow med.
1 zinc yellow hue

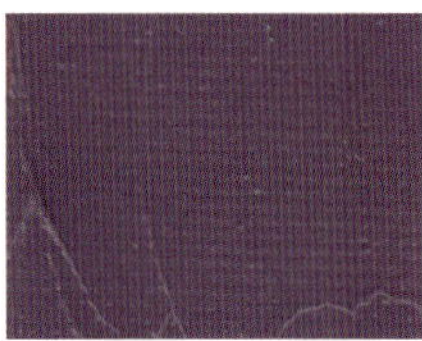

294. 3 magenta
1 white

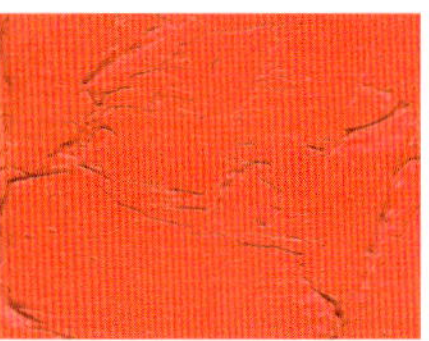

295. 1 white
1 cadmium vermilion

296. 20 white
1 alizarin crimson

297. 8 white
8 Thalo® red rose
4 cobalt violet hue

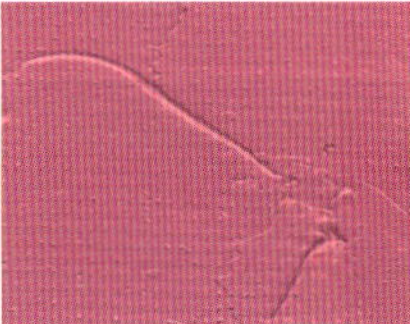

298. 8 white
8 Thalo® red rose
1 cobalt violet hue

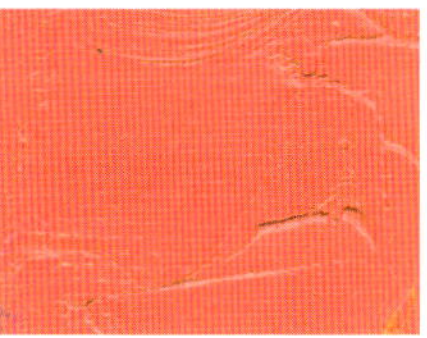

299. 7 white
1 cadmium red light

300. 1 white
1 zinc yellow hue

LandscapeColorRecipes

COLORS USED

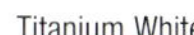
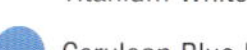
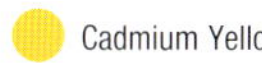
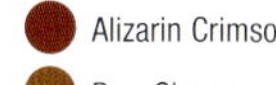

- Titanium White
- Cerulean Blue Hue
- Burnt Umber
- Cadmium Vermilion
- Cadmium Yellow Med.
- Permanent Blue
- Naples Yellow Hue
- Yellow Ochre
- Ivory Black
- Viridian Green
- Cadmium Yellow Light
- Permanent Green Light
- Zinc Yellow Hue
- Cadmium Red Light
- Cadmium Orange
- Raw Umber
- Alizarin Crimson
- Raw Sienna

301. 5 white
5 Naples yellow hue
3 cadmium yellow light

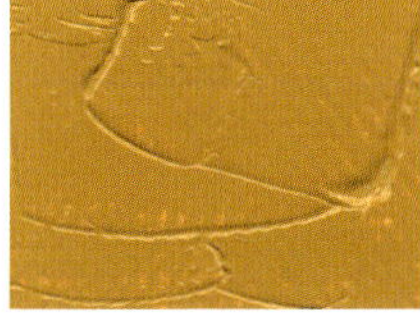

302. 1 cadmium yellow med.
1 • viridian green

303. 3 Naples yellow hue
1 • cadmium orange
1 • cerulean blue hue

304. 6 Naples yellow hue
1 cadmium orange
1 white

305. 1 white
1 permanent blue
2 • alizarin crimson
2 • burnt umber

306. 1 #305
1 • alizarin crimson

307. 1 cadmium orange
1 cerulean blue hue

308. 3 Naples yellow hue
1 cadmium orange
4 • cerulean blue hue

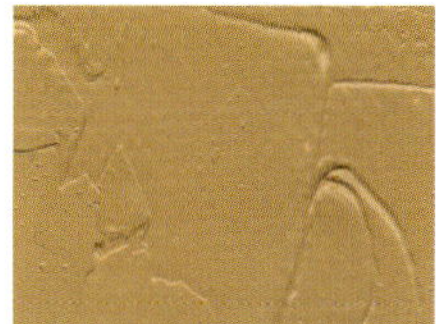

309. 5 white
3 yellow ochre
2 • permanent blue

310. 4 white
2 Naples yellow hue
1 cadmium yellow light

311. 1 white
2 • raw sienna
2 • zinc yellow hue

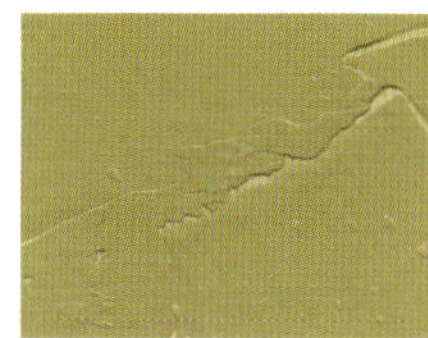

312. 1 white
2 • cadmium orange
3 • permanent green light

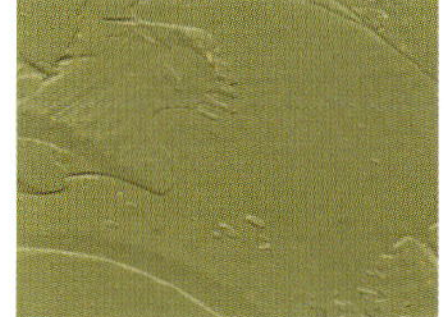

313. 1 white
3 cadmium orange
6 permanent green light

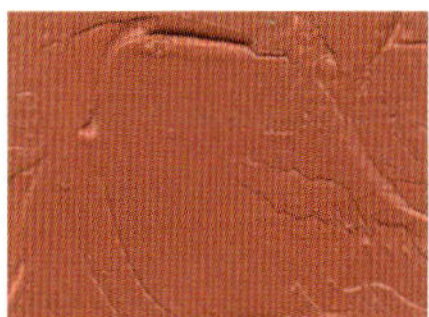

314. 1 white
3 cadmium vermilion
1 • ivory black

315. 2 cadmium vermilion
1 ivory black

316. 4 white
1 cadmium orange
3 permanent green light

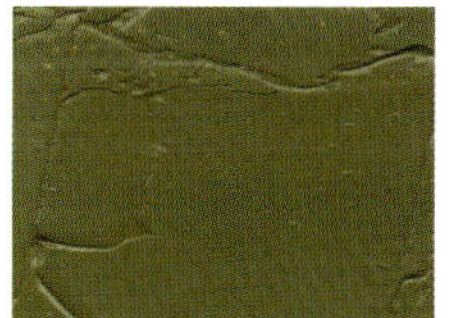

317. 1 cadmium orange
3 permanent green light
1 white

318. 3 permanent green light
2 • cadmium red light

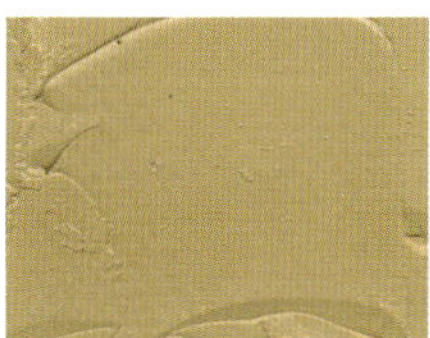

319. 2 white
1 yellow ochre
2 • cerulean blue hue

320. 8 white
1 raw umber
1 • permanent blue
1 • yellow ochre

Landscape Color Recipes

COLORS USED

- Titanium White
- Raw Sienna
- Alizarin Crimson
- Ivory Black
- Burnt Umber
- Naples Yellow Hue
- Raw Umber
- Thalo® Green (Blue Shade)
- Thalo® Blue
- Cobalt Violet Hue
- Permanent Blue
- Thalo® Red Rose
- Cerulean Blue Hue

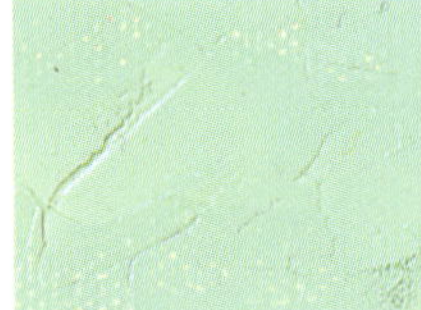

321. 1 white
1 • Thalo® green
(blue shade)

322. 2 white
1 ivory black
6 cerulean blue hue

323. 1 white
2 • Thalo® blue
1 raw sienna

324. 3 cerulean blue hue
1 white
2 • alizarin crimson

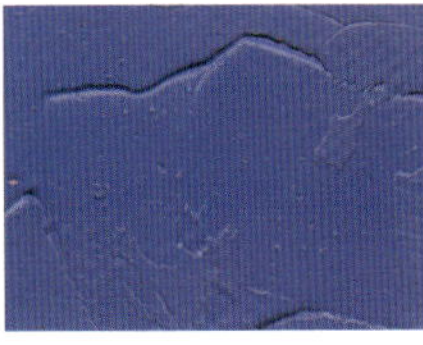

325. 2 white
3 permanent blue
2 • Thalo® red rose

326. 2 white
1 • Thalo® blue

327. 1 cerulean blue hue
1 permanent blue
1 white

328. 1 #327
1 • raw umber

329. 2 white
1 permanent blue
1 • burnt umber
1 • alizarin crimson

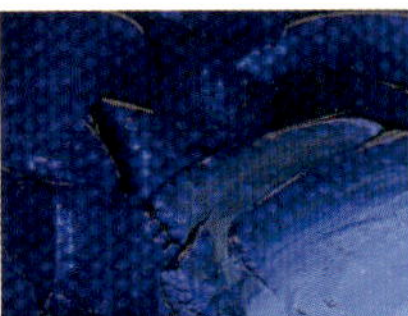

330. permanent blue (pure)

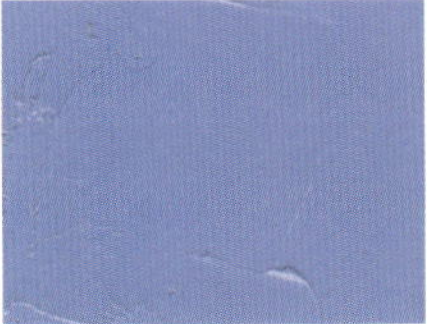

331. 1 permanent blue
1 white
2 • Thalo® red rose

332. 1 white
4 • cobalt violet hue
1 • permanent blue

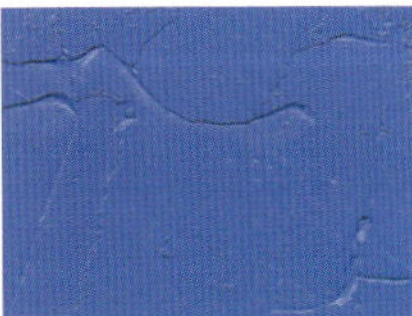

333. 2 permanent blue
1 cerulean blue hue
1 white

334. 1 #333
1 • burnt umber
1 • alizarin crimson

335. 2 white
1 Naples yellow hue
2 • Thalo® blue
1 • burnt umber

COLORS USED

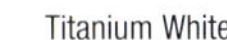

Titanium White
Burnt Sienna
Alizarin Crimson
Permanent Green Light
Burnt Umber
Naples Yellow Hue
Ivory Black
Cerulean Blue Hue
Cadmium Orange
Cobalt Violet Hue
Cadmium Yellow Medium
Permanent Blue
Raw Sienna
Venetian Red

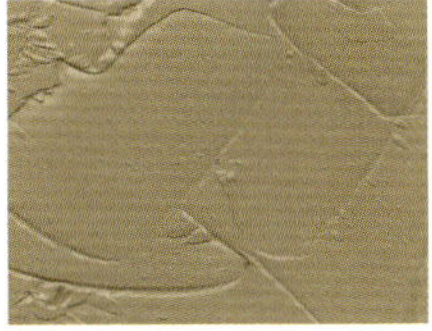

336. 6 white
1 burnt umber

337. 2 white
1 burnt umber
6 • cerulean blue hue

338. 1 white
2 • burnt sienna

339. 1 white
2 • cadmium orange
1 • cerulean blue hue

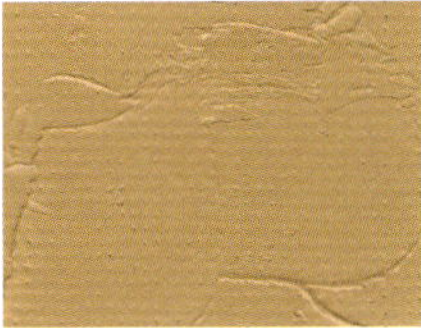

340. 3 white
1 raw sienna
1 • permanent blue

341. 1 #340
1 • burnt sienna
1• permanent blue

342. 1 white
1 • cadmium orange
2 • Naples yellow hue

343. 1 white
3 • Naples yellow hue
1 • cobalt violet hue

344. 3 white
1 alizarin crimson
1 permanent blue

345. 1 #344
2 white
2 • cadmium orange

346. 1 #344
2 • ivory black
2 • permanent blue

347. 3 white
1 #345
1 • cadmium orange

348. 4 cadmium yellow medium
2 cobalt violet hue
2 • permanent blue

349. 1 Venetian red
5 Naples yellow hue
1 permanent green light

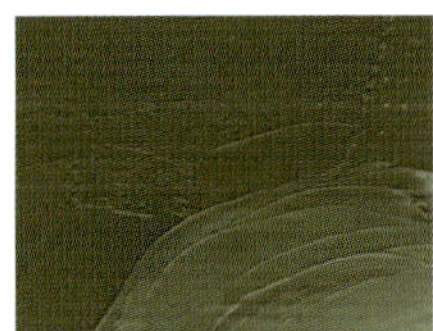

350. 2 cerulean blue hue
1 cadmium orange

LandscapeColorRecipes

COLORS USED

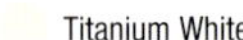

- Titanium White
- Raw Sienna
- Viridian Green
- Cadmium Yellow Medium
- Cadmium Orange
- Naples Yellow Hue
- Cadmium Vermilion
- Thalo® Green (Blue Shade)
- Cadmium Red Light
- Burnt Sienna
- Permanent Blue
- Thalo® Red Rose
- Cadmium Yellow Light

351. 16 white
1 cadmium orange
1 Naples yellow hue

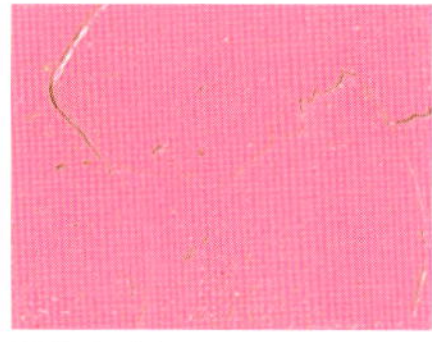

352. 1 white
3 • Thalo® red rose

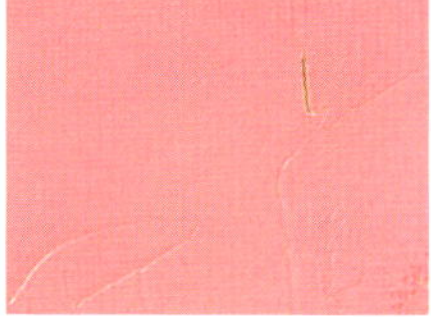

353. 2 white
1 • cadmium vermilion

354. 3 white
1 • burnt sienna

355. 2 white
1 • cadmium yellow med.

356. 2 white
2 • Naples yellow hue
1 • viridian green

357. 2 white
1 • Thalo® green (blue shade)
3 • Naples yellow hue

358. 2 white
4 • Naples yellow hue
2 • viridian green

359. 1 #355
2 white
1 • permanent blue

360. 2 white
2 • cadmium yellow med.
2 • Naples yellow hue

361. 2 white
2 • raw sienna

362. 4 white
1 • raw sienna

363. 1 white
2 Naples yellow hue
1 • cadmium red light

364. 1 #363
1 Naples yellow hue
1 • cadmium yellow med.

365. 1 white
2 • Naples yellow hue
3 • cadmium yellow light

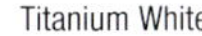

COLORS USED

Titanium White
Burnt Sienna
Yellow Ochre
Burnt Umber
Naples Yellow Hue
Ivory Black
Raw Umber
Cadmium Orange
Venetian Red
Permanent Blue
Raw Sienna

366. 2 white
1 raw umber
1 cadmium orange

367. 1 #366
1 white

368. 3 white
1 raw umber

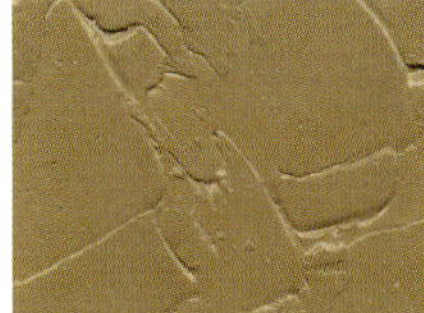

369. 2 #368
1 yellow ochre
1 white

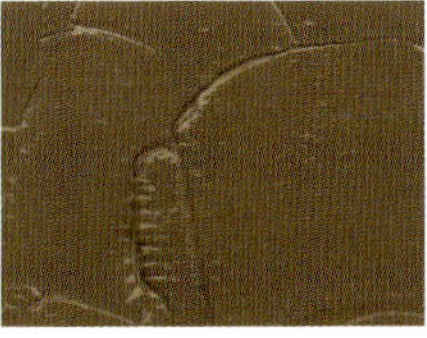

370. 2 white
1 burnt umber
1 • cadmium orange

371. 6 white
1 raw umber

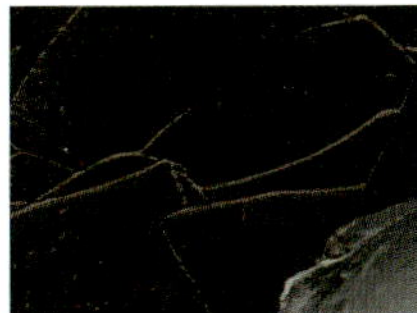

372. 2 ivory black
1 permanent blue

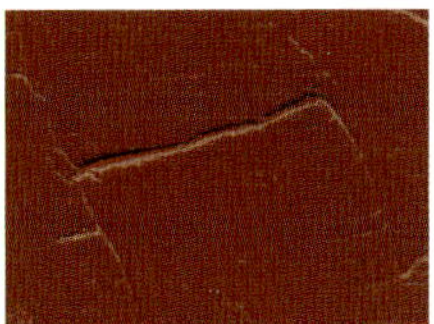

373. 2 burnt sienna
1 Venetian red
4 raw sienna

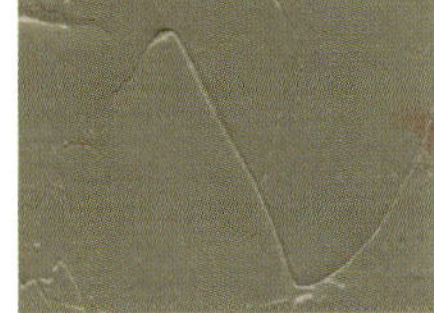

374. 3 white
1 burnt umber
1 • cadmium orange
4 • permanent blue

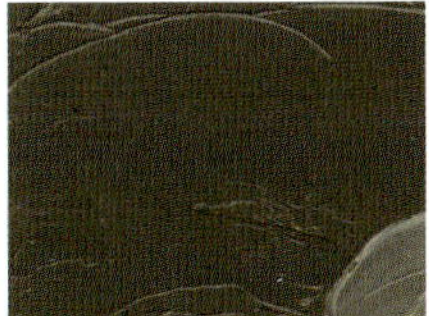

375. 2 ivory black
1 burnt umber
1 white

376. 1 #373
2 Naples yellow hue
1 white

377. 7 white
2 burnt umber
1 raw sienna

378. 3 white
1 burnt sienna
1 burnt umber

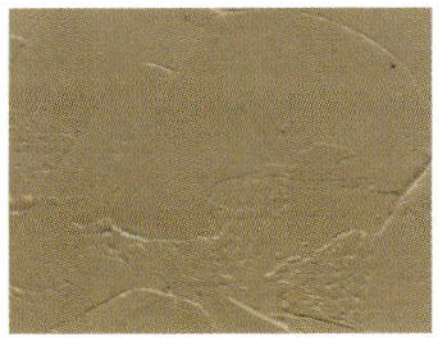

379. 1 #378
2 white
2 • permanent blue

380. 2 white
2 yellow ochre
1 • burnt umber

LandscapeColorRecipes

COLORS USED

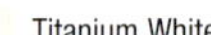

Titanium White	Burnt Umber	Thalo® Green (Blue Shade)	Permanent Blue
Thalo® Blue	Naples Yellow Hue	Thalo® Red Rose	Viridian Green
Alizarin Crimson	Cobalt Blue	Cobalt Violet Hue	Cadmium Yellow Medium
Cadmium Orange	Yellow Ochre	Zinc Yellow Hue	Cadmium Red Light

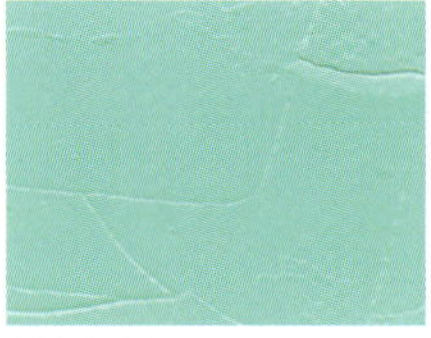

381. 2 white
1 • Thalo® green (blue shade)

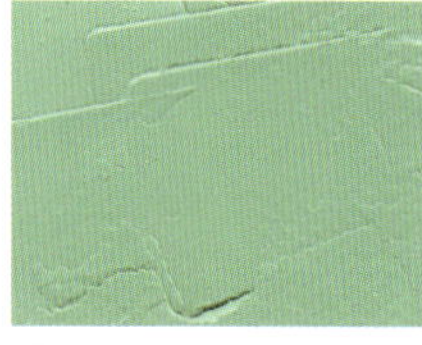

382. 2 white
1 • Thalo® green (blue shade)
3 • Naples yellow hue
1 • burnt umber

383. 2 white
1 • Thalo® blue
1 • burnt umber

384. 8 white
1 • Thalo® green (blue shade)

385. 3 white
1 • burnt umber
2 • permanent blue

386. 1 white
2 • cobalt blue
1 • cadmium red light

387. 12 white
1 cadmium orange
1 • Thalo® red rose

388. 4 white
1 • cadmium orange
1 • zinc yellow hue

389. 6 white
2 yellow ochre
1 permanent blue

390. 2 white
1 #389
1 yellow ochre

391. 8 white
1 cadmium yellow medium
1 • viridian green

392. 2 white
1 cadmium yellow medium
1 • cobalt violet hue

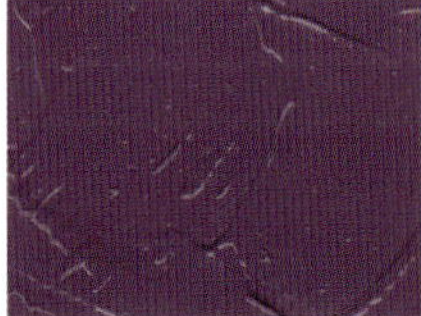

393. 1 white
4 Thalo® red rose
3 cobalt violet hue
1 permanent blue

394. 1 white
6 cobalt violet hue
1 permanent blue

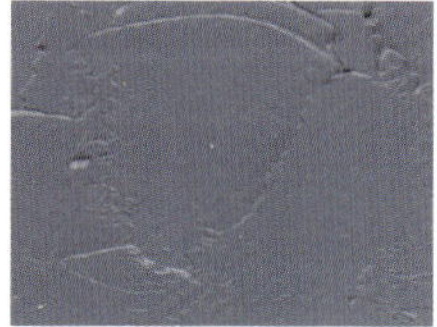

395. 2 white
1 permanent blue
3 • alizarin crimson
2 • burnt umber

COLORS USED

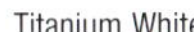

- Titanium White
- Burnt Sienna
- Alizarin Crimson
- Zinc Yellow Hue
- Burnt Umber
- Naples Yellow Hue
- Cadmium Red Light
- Cadmium Yellow Light
- Cerulean Blue Hue
- Cadmium Orange
- Cobalt Violet Hue
- Thalo® Red Rose
- Permanent Blue
- Yellow Ochre
- Viridian Green

396. 1 burnt umber
1 alizarin crimson
2 white

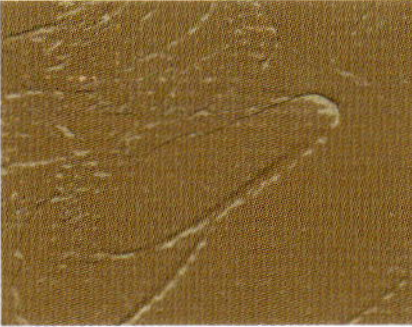

397. 2 #396
2 yellow ochre
1 white

398. 2 #396
1 permanent blue

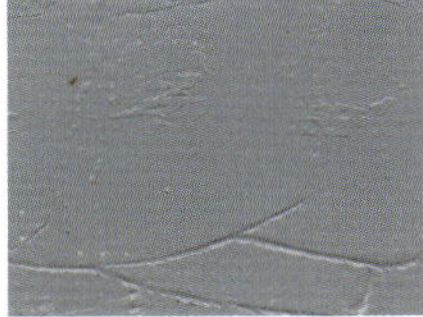

399. 2 white
1 permanent blue
2 • cadmium red light

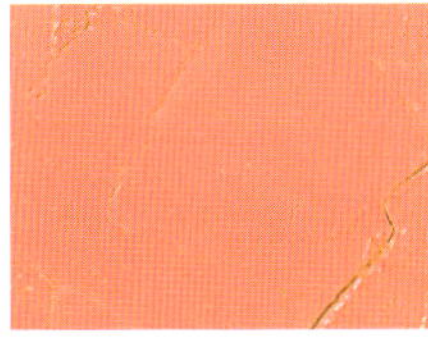

400. 2 white
1 • cadmium red light
2 • Naples yellow hue

401. 2 white
1 • cadmium red light
1 • permanent blue

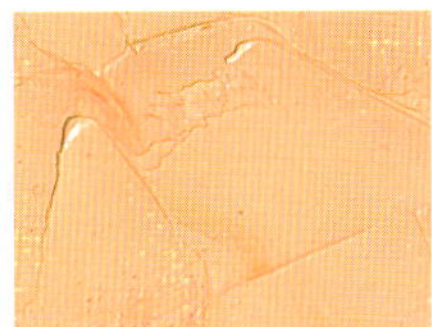

402. 1 white
1 • cadmium orange

403. 2 zinc yellow hue
4 cobalt violet hue

404. 8 cerulean blue hue
12 Naples yellow hue
1 cadmium orange

405. 2 Naples yellow hue
1 • cerulean blue hue
1 • cadmium orange

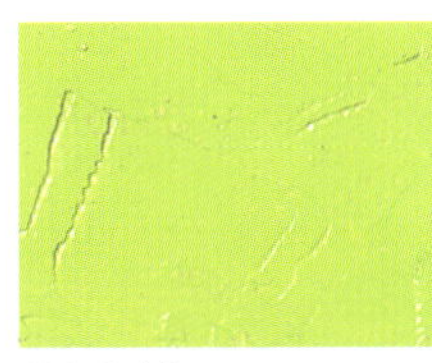

406. 5 white
1 cadmium yellow light
2 • cerulean blue hue

407. 4 white
6 cadmium yellow light
2 cerulean blue hue
1 viridian green

408. 2 Naples yellow hue
2 burnt sienna
1 • cadmium red light

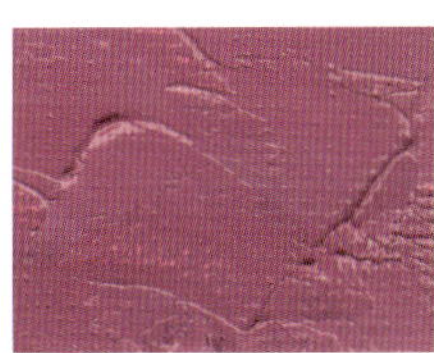

409. 4 white
6 Thalo® red rose
4 cobalt violet hue

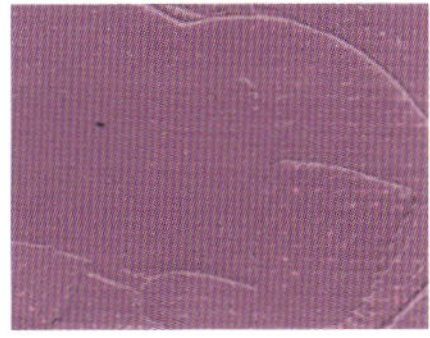

410. 1 white
5 Thalo® red rose
4 cobalt violet hue

LandscapeColorRecipes

COLORS USED

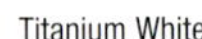
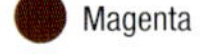
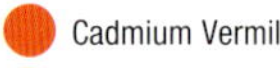
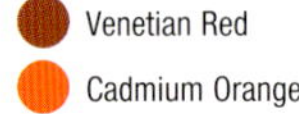

- Titanium White
- Raw Sienna
- Alizarin Crimson
- Zinc Yellow Hue
- Magenta
- Cadmium Red Light
- Ivory Black
- Cadmium Vermilion
- Thalo® Red Rose
- Cobalt Violet Hue
- Venetian Red
- Cadmium Orange
- Cadmium Yellow Light

411. 4 white
5 cobalt violet hue
1 • Thalo® red rose

412. 15 white
1 magenta

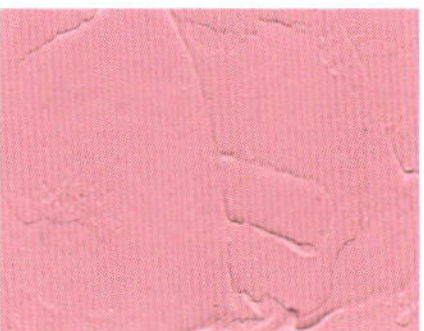

413. 5 white
1 Thalo® red rose
3 • cobalt violet hue

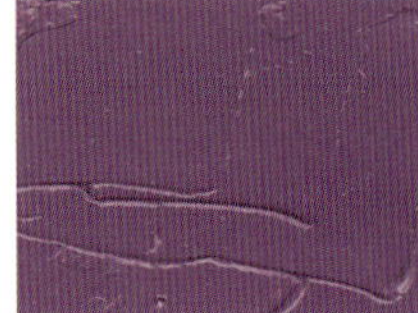

414. 4 cobalt violet hue
1 white
1 • Thalo® red rose

415. 1 white
3 alizarin crimson

416. 3 white
1 Venetian red

417. 1 cadmium red light
1 raw sienna

418. 2 cadmium vermilion
1 alizarin crimson

419. 2 white
4 cadmium red light

420. 2 cadmium red light
1 cadmium vermilion

421. 2 white
1 • cadmium red light
1 • cadmium orange

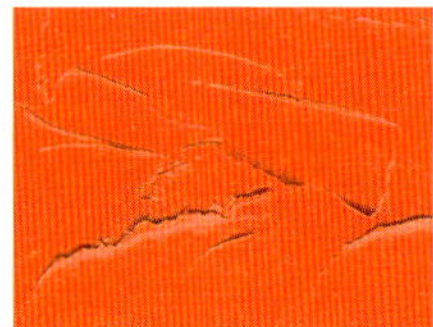

422. 2 white
4 cadmium red light
6 zinc yellow hue

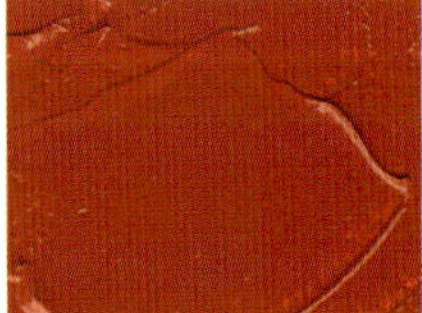

423. 7 alizarin crimson
9 cadmium yellow light
1 white

424. 3 cadmium red light
1 ivory black

425. 1 cadmium red light
1 white
2 • ivory black

LandscapeColorRecipes

COLORS USED

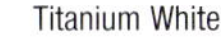

- Titanium White
- Yellow Ochre
- Alizarin Crimson
- Burnt Umber
- Naples Yellow Hue
- Zinc Yellow Hue
- Cadmium Yellow Light
- Cadmium Orange
- Cadmium Red Light
- Permanent Blue
- Thalo® Red Rose
- Cadmium Yellow Medium

426. 2 yellow ochre
1 cadmium red light
3 cadmium yellow light

427. 2 cadmium orange
2 • alizarin crimson

428. 1 cadmium orange
2 • cadmium yellow light

429. 4 white
3 cadmium orange

430. 10 white
2 cadmium orange
1 zinc yellow hue

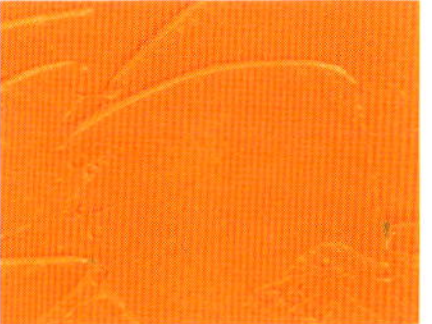

431. 5 cadmium yellow light
1 cadmium orange

432. 1 cadmium orange
1 Naples yellow hue

433. 1 cadmium orange
1 Naples yellow hue
1 cadmium yellow light

434. 1 cadmium orange
2 • burnt umber

435. 9 zinc yellow hue
2 cadmium orange

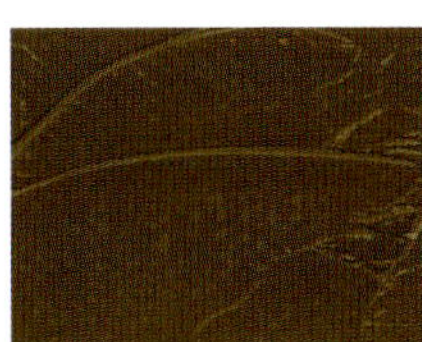

436. 3 cadmium orange
1 permanent blue

437. 8 white
2 cadmium red light
14 zinc yellow hue

438. 1 #437
2 • cadmium red light

439. 2 cadmium orange
2 • Thalo® red rose

440. 2 cadmium yellow medium
1 • cadmium orange

LandscapeColorRecipes

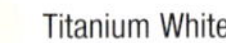

COLORS USED

- Titanium White
- Burnt Sienna
- Alizarin Crimson
- Ivory Black
- Burnt Umber
- Naples Yellow Hue
- Cadmium Orange
- Cadmium Red Light
- Zinc Yellow Hue
- Cadmium Vermilion
- Cobalt Violet Hue
- Cadmium Yellow Light
- Permanent Blue
- Venetian Red
- Cerulean Blue Hue

441. 2 zinc yellow hue
1 cerulean blue hue
1 cadmium orange

442. 8 cereulean blue hue
12 Naples yellow hue
1 cadmium orange

443. 1 white
1 cadmium yellow light
1 • ivory black

444. 3 white
1 permanent blue
5 cobalt violet hue

445. 6 cobalt violet hue
1 white

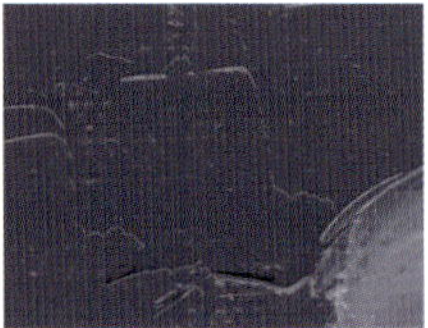

446. 1 burnt umber
1 alizarin crimson
4 permanent blue
3 white

447. 2 white
1 ivory black
1 • cadmium vermilion

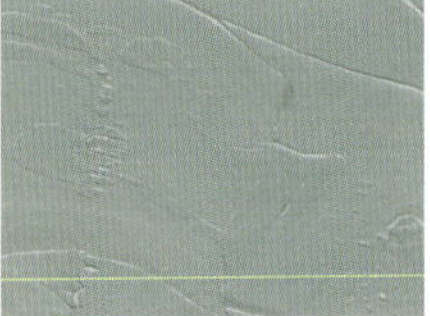

448. 1 white
3 • permanent blue
1 • burnt umber

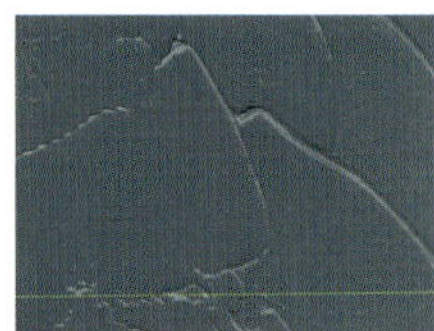

449. 5 permanent blue
3 white
1 burnt umber

450. 1 #447
2 • cerulean blue hue

451. 2 white
2 permanent blue
1 alizarin crimson

452. 1 white
1 Venetian red
3 permanent blue

453. 1 cadmium orange
2 cerulean blue hue

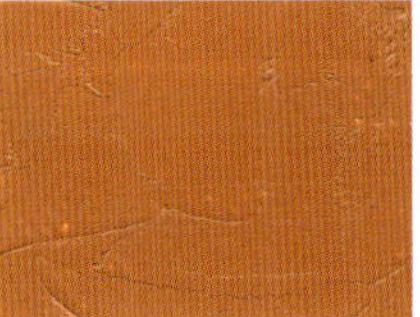

454. 2 white
12 Naples yellow hue
1 cadmium red light
2 burnt sienna

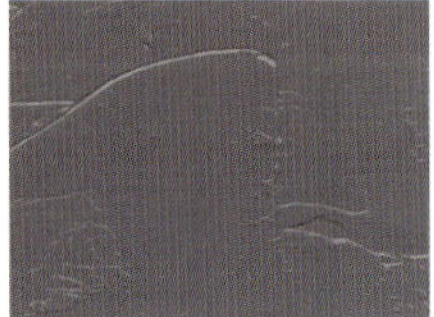

455. 1 burnt umber
1 alizarin crimson
2 permanent blue
6 white

COLORS USED

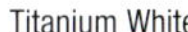
Titanium White
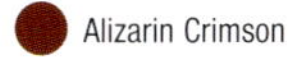
Alizarin Crimson
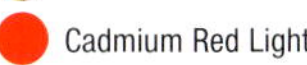
Cadmium Red Light
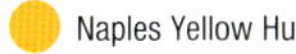
Naples Yellow Hue
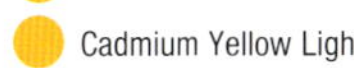
Cadmium Yellow Light
Cerulean Blue Hue
Cadmium Yellow Medium
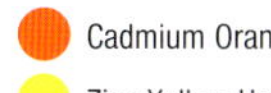
Cadmium Orange
Zinc Yellow Hue

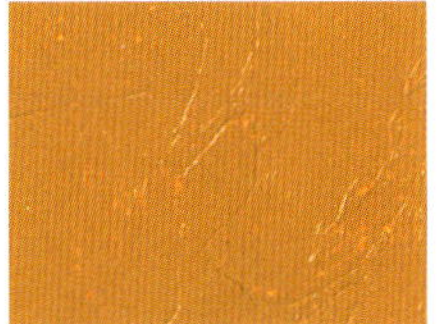

456. 3 Naples yellow hue
1 • cadmium orange
1 • cerulean blue hue

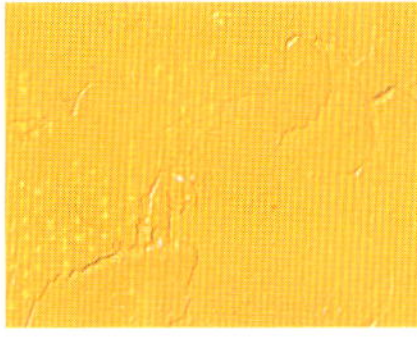

457. 4 white
4 Naples yellow hue
1 cadmium yellow light

458. 4 white
1 Naples yellow hue
2 • cadmium yellow light

459. 6 white
1 Naples yellow hue
1 • cadmium yellow light

460. 4 white
3 Naples yellow hue
1 • cerulean blue hue

461. 1 white
1 cadmium yellow light

462. 1 white
1 zinc yellow hue

463. 5 white
1 cadmium yellow medium

464. 3 white
1 cadmium yellow medium

465. 7 zinc yellow hue
2 cadmium orange

466. 4 white
1.5 cadmium orange

467. 1.5 white
2 cadmium yellow medium

468. 8 white
2 cadmium red light
4 zinc yellow hue

469. 2 #468
1 cadmium red light

470. 11 white
3 alizarin crimson
5 cadmium yellow light

Landscape Color Recipes

COLORS USED

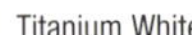

- Titanium White
- Yellow Ochre
- Alizarin Crimson
- Ivory Black
- Burnt Umber
- Naples Yellow Hue
- Cadmium Orange
- Cadmium Red Light
- Permanent Green Light
- Cadmium Vermilion
- Cobalt Violet Hue
- Cadmium Yellow Light
- Permanent Blue
- Cadmium Yellow Medium
- Cerulean Blue Hue

471. 2 alizarin crimson
1 cadmium red light

472. 5 cadmium orange
1 cerulean blue hue

473. 3 white
1 ivory black
2 cadmium vermilion
2 • cadmium orange

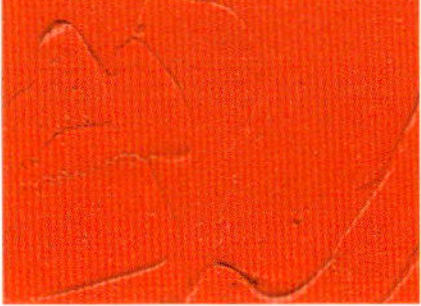

474. 1 white
1.5 cadmium vermilion
1 • cadmium red light

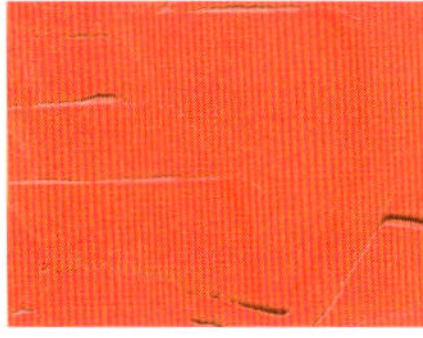

475. 3 white
1 cadmium vermilion
1 • cadmium red light

476. 2 cadmium red light
2 permanent green light
1 burnt umber

477. 1 Naples yellow hue
2 • #476
2 • white

478. 1 #477
1.5 white

479. 1 cadmium yellow medium
3 cobalt violet hue

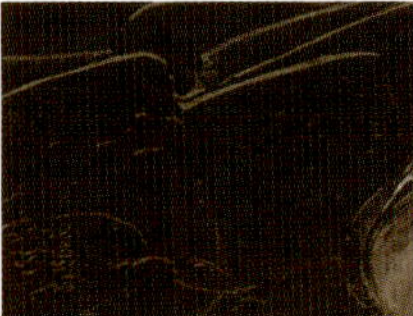

480. 2 ivory black
1 alizarin crimson
3 Naples yellow hue

481. 4 white
2 ivory black
1 cerulean blue hue

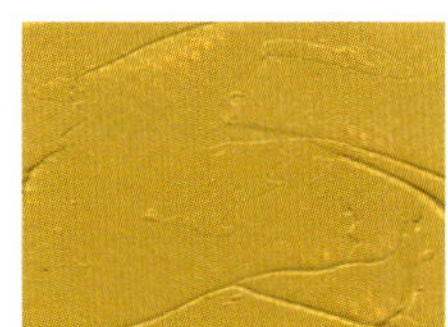

482. 2 cadmium yellow light
1 • ivory black

483. 4 cadmium yellow light
1 ivory black

484. 4 white
1 cadmium orange
3 permanent green light

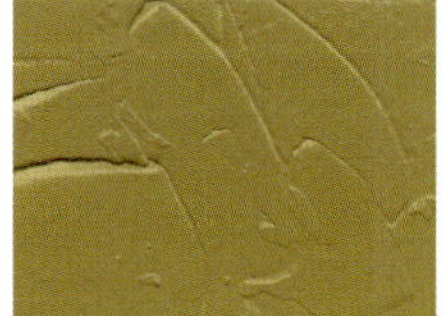

485. 6 white
3 yellow ochre
1 permanent blue

COLORS USED

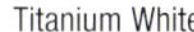
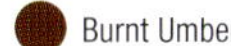

- Titanium White
- Viridian green
- Alizarin Crimson
- Burnt Umber
- Naples Yellow Hue
- Ivory Black
- Cerulean Blue Hue
- Cadmium Yellow Light
- Thalo® Red Rose
- Permanent Blue
- Thalo® Blue
- Zinc Yellow Hue

486. 1 white
3 permanent blue
1 • ivory black
1 • alizarin crimson

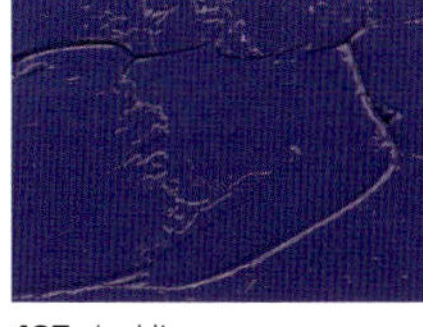

487. 1 white
4 permanent blue
2 Thalo® red rose

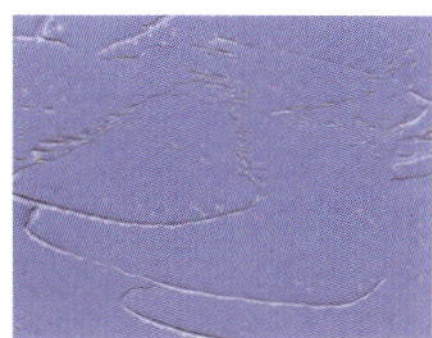

488. 2 white
1 #487

489. 1 white
2 Thalo® red rose
1 permanent blue

490. 1 cerulean blue hue
1 permanent blue

491. 2 cerulean blue hue
1 ivory black

492. 2 white
1 permanent blue
1 • burnt umber

493. 1 #492
1 white

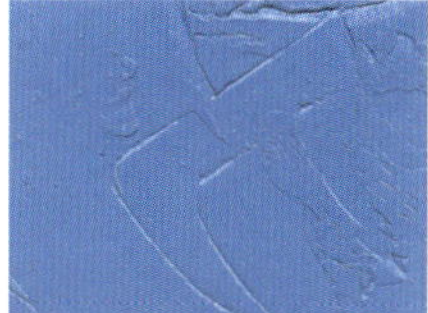

494. 1 cerulean blue hue
1 permanent blue
2 white

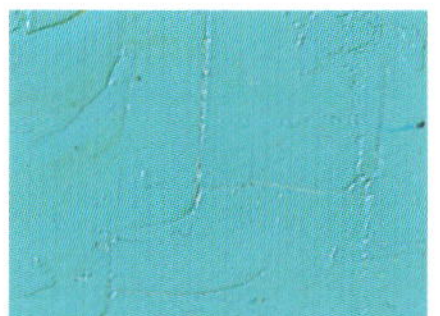

495. 1 white
1 • Thalo® blue
2 • Naples yellow hue

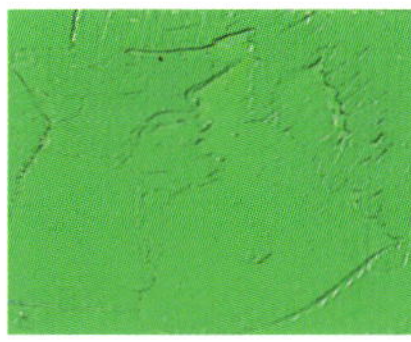

496. 2 #495
1 cadmium yellow light

497. 1 white
1 cadmium yellow light
1 viridian green

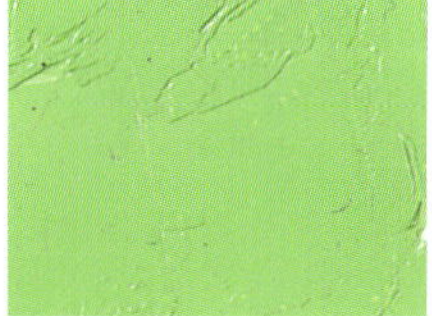

498. 1 #497
2 white

499. 1 white
2 • viridian green

500. 1 #499
2 white
1 • zinc yellow hue

Landscape Color Recipes

COLORS USED

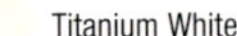
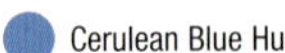
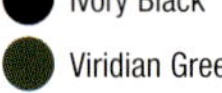

- Titanium White
- Cerulean Blue Hue
- Alizarin Crimson
- Venetian Red
- Naples Yellow Hue
- Cadmium Red Llight
- Cadmium Yellow Medium
- Zinc Yellow Hue
- Cadmium Yellow Light
- Ivory Black
- Viridian Green

501. 1 white
3 • Naples yellow hue

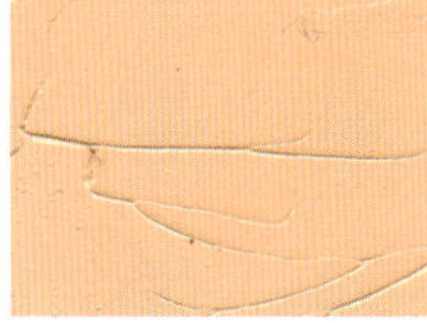

502. 5 #501
1 • Venetian red

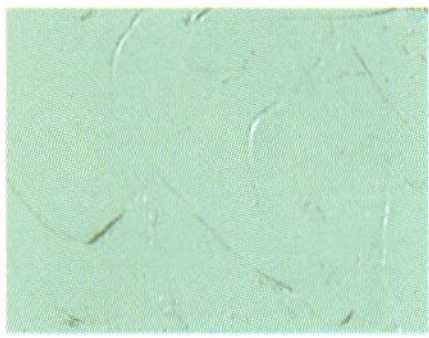

503. 1 white
1 #502
2 • cerulean blue hue

504. 1 white
3 #503
1 • cadmium red light
1 • ivory black

505. 2 white
1 • cadmium yellow light

506. 1 #505
2 Naples yellow hue

507. 1 #506
1 • alizarin crimson

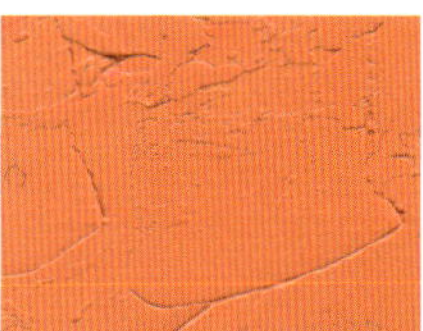

508. 1 #507
1 • alizarin crimson

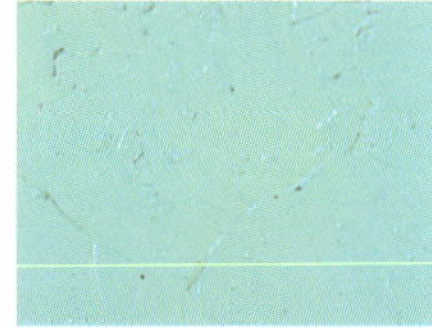

509. 2 white
3 • cerulean blue hue
1 • viridian green

510. 1 white
4 • viridian green
2 • cadmium red light

511. 1 white
3 • cerulean blue hue

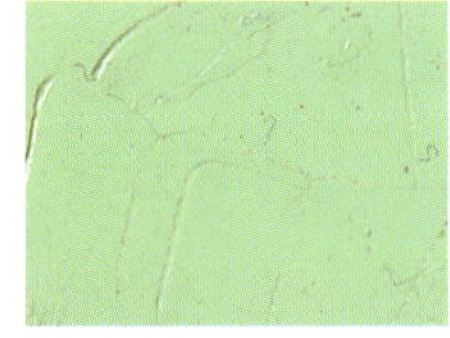

512. 2 white
1 #511
1 • cadmium yellow med.

513. 1 white
1 #512
1 • zinc yellow hue

514. 2 white
1 cadmium yellow medium

515. 1 #514
3 • cadmium red light
1 • alizarin crimson

COLORS USED

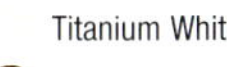
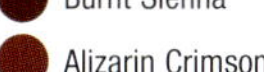

- Titanium White
- Burnt Sienna
- Alizarin Crimson
- Burnt Umber
- Naples Yellow Hue
- Cadmium Yellow Light
- Cadmium Yellow Medium
- Cadmium Orange
- Yellow Ochre
- Zinc Yellow Hue

516. 1 cadmium yellow light
2 • white

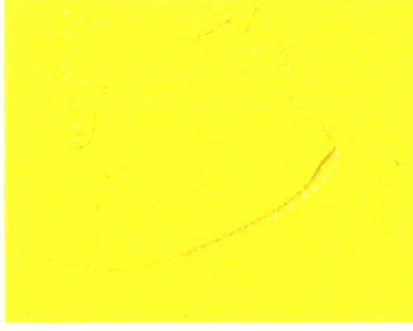

517. 1 zinc yellow hue
2 • white

518. 2 white
1 zinc yellow hue
1 • cadmium orange

519. 2 cadmium yellow light
1 • burnt umber

520. 3 zinc yellow hue
1 • burnt umber

521. 2 cadmium yellow medium
1 • burnt umber

522. 5 cadmium yellow medium
1 • alizarin crimson

523. 2 cadmium yellow light
1 Naples yellow hue
1 white

524. 2 cadmium yellow light
1 • burnt sienna

525. 2 cadmium yellow light
1 • cadmium orange

526. 2 white
1 #525

527. 1 #523
1 #525

528. 4 white
1 Naples yellow hue

529. 5 white
1 yellow ochre

530. 14 white
1 cadmium yellow medium
1 zinc yellow hue

ColorGuidanceIndex

LEGEND

+ Mix listed recipe colors together for one resultant color
& Use all listed color mixes individually on the scene
, Multiple recipes separated by a comma indicates a variation of selections

LEGEND

+ Mix listed recipe colors together for one resultant color
& Use all listed color mixes individually on the scene
, Multiple recipes separated by a comma indicates a variation of selections

G

H

I

J

K

L

M

ColorGuidanceIndex

LEGEND

\+ Mix listed recipe colors together for one resultant color
& Use all listed color mixes individually on the scene
, Multiple recipes separated by a comma indicates a variation of selections

N

O

P

Q

R

LEGEND

+ Mix listed recipe colors together for one resultant color
& Use all listed color mixes individually on the scene
, Multiple recipes separated by a comma indicates a variation of selections

S

ColorGuidanceIndex

LEGEND

\+ Mix listed recipe colors together for one resultant color
& Use all listed color mixes individually on the scene
, Multiple recipes separated by a comma indicates a variation of selections

- Daybreak Pinkish Clouds
  - Main Color 72
  - Highlight Color 65, 74
  - Shadow Color 70
- Daybreak Pale Sky
  - Zenith 111
  - Secondary Color 74
  - Horizon Color 118
- Daybreak Pale Sky Clouds
  - Main Color 77
  - Highlight Color 118
  - Shadow Color 67
- Dusk Blue Sky
  - Zenith 75
  - Secondary Color 76
  - Horizon Color 65, 77
- Dusk Blue Sky Clouds
  - Main Color 78
  - Highlight Color 79
  - Shadow Color 80
- Early Morning Cool Sky
  - Zenith 109
  - Secondary Color 110
  - Horizon Color 108, 111
- Early Morning Cool Sky Clouds
  - Main Color 111
  - Highlight Color 108
  - Shadow Color 112
- Early Morning Warm Sky
  - Zenith 123
  - Secondary Color 124
  - Horizon Color 121, 123, 124
- Early Morning Warm Sky Clouds
  - Main Color 77
  - Highlight Color 108
  - Shadow Color 101
- Morning Blue Sky
  - Zenith 106
  - Secondary Color 110
  - Horizon Color 111
- Morning Blue Sky Clouds
  - Main Color 74
  - Highlight Color 108
  - Shadow Color 68
- Afternoon Cumulus Sky
  - Zenith 125
  - Secondary Color 126
  - Horizon Color 127
- Afternoon Cumulus Sky Clouds
  - Main Color 129
  - Highlight Color 130
  - Shadow Color 128
- Afternoon Warm Sky
  - Zenith 106
  - Secondary Color 114
  - Horizon Color 108, 111
- Afternoon Warm Sky Clouds
  - Main Color 118
  - Highlight Color 108
  - Shadow Color 110, 117
- Evening Sky, Clouds & Light Rays
  - Zenith 114, 115
  - Secondary Color 114
  - Horizon Clouds 116
- Evening Sky Clouds
  - Main Color 114
  - Highlight Color 108
  - Shadow Color 116
  - Light Rays Blended 108
- Rising Sun, Reddish Clouds
  - Sky Zenith 511
  - Middle Sky 512
  - Lower Sky 513
  - Cloud Glow 515
  - Cloud Highlight 514
  - Cloud Shadow 510
- Sunset Sky – Low Sun
  - Zenith 136
  - Sun Center 105
  - Sun Perimeter 131
  - Primary Glow 132
  - Secondary Glow 133
- Sunset Sky – Low Sun Clouds
  - Bottom Glow 134
  - Middle Color 134, 135
  - Top Shadow Color 135
- Sunset Sky – Dramatic Sky, Horizon Sun
  - Zenith 124
  - Secondary Color 113+124
  - Horizon Color 113
- Sunset Sky – Dramatic Clouds
  - Main Color 146
  - Highlight Color 133 & 145
  - Shadow Color 147
- Sunset Sky – Warm Orange
  - Zenith 143
  - Secondary Glow Color 142
  - Sun/Horizon Color 131
- Sunset Sky – Warm Orange Clouds
  - Main Color 141
  - Highlight Color 65
  - Shadow Color 144
- Sunset Sky, Purplish
  - Zenith 138
  - Secondary Color 137
  - Sun/Horizon Color 139
- Sunset Clouds, Purplish
  - Main Color 141
  - Highlight Color 129
  - Shadow Color 140
- Sunset, Reddish Sky
  - Zenith 113 & 17
- Secondary Color 5 & 117
  - Horizon Color 113 & 17
- Sunset Clouds Reddish
  - Main Color 17
  - Highlight Color 5, 113
  - Shadow Color 109, 17
- Moonlight Sky
  - Moon 148
  - Moon Inner Glow 150
  - Moon Outer Glow 149
  - Outer Sky 151
- Moonlight Sky Clouds
  - Main Color 152
  - Highlight Color 148 & 153
- Stormy Gray Sky
  - Main Gray Color 154
  - Clouds Dark Color 155
  - Clouds Accent Dark 156
  - Light Glow Through Clouds 157 & 158
- Mood Skies
  - Misty Sun
    - Sun 118
    - Glow 105
    - Sky 107
  - Grayish
    - Sun 5
    - Glow 117
    - Sky 68
  - Soft Greens
    - Sun 65
    - Glow 74
    - Outer Sky 111
  - Hot Yellow Orange
    - Sun 5
    - Glow 59
    - Sky 50
  - Low Setting Sun
    - Sun 505
    - Inner Glow 506
    - Outer Glow 507
    - Clouds 510
  - Pastel Dawn
    - Horizon 501
    - Middle Sky 502
    - Zenith 503
    - Clouds 504
  - Pink with Low Light
    - Horizon 65
    - Middle sky 117
    - Zenith 60
- Sky Blues (General)
  - Afternoon Warm 105
  - Evening Dusk 75, 76, 115
  - Midday Bright 121, 122
  - Morning 110
  - Spring Fresh 114
  - Twilight Blue 110
- Smog
  - Gray 389
  - Tannish 390

LEGEND

+ Mix listed recipe colors together for one resultant color
& Use all listed color mixes individually on the scene
, Multiple recipes separated by a comma indicates a variation of selections

T

LEGEND

+ Mix listed recipe colors together for one resultant color
& Use all listed color mixes individually on the scene
, Multiple recipes separated by a comma indicates a variation of selections

Basic 155
Secondary 155 + 156
Dark 156
Light 154
Birch Tree (Paper)
Foliage Colors
Dark 185
Medium 186
Light 187
Trunk Colors
Bark (Peeling in strips)
Basic 168
Secondary 166 + 168
Dark 166
Light 165
Blue Spruce Tree
Foliage Colors
Dark 173
Medium 174
Light 163
Trunk Colors
Bark (Scaly Dark Gray)
Basic 38
Secondary 38 + 26
Dark 26
Light 56
Buckeye Tree (Ohio)
Foliage Colors
Dark 226
Medium 227
Light 229
Trunk Colors
Bark (Fissured & Scaly)
Basic 207
Secondary 207 + 216
Dark 216
Light 208
Cedar Tree
Foliage Colors
Dark 81
Medium 98
Light 100
Trunk Colors
Bark (Ridged & Furrowed)
Basic 44
Secondary 44 + 26
Dark 26
Light 40
Cherry Tree (Black)
Foliage Colors
Dark 225
Medium 226
Light 227
Trunk Colors
Bark (Young, reddish brown with lenticels, Old, scaly lenticels brown/black)
Basic 224
Dark 222
Light 223
Blossom Pink 287
Chestnut Tree (American)
Foliage Colors
Dark 161
Medium 162
Light 163
Trunk Colors
Bark (Flat scaly ridges)
Basic 217
Secondary 217 + 216
Dark 216
Light 215
Cottonwood Tree
Foliage Colors
Dark 225
Medium 228
Light 229
Trunk Colors
Bark (Ridged, furrowed)
Basic 217
Secondary 217 + 218
Dark 216
Light 218
Cypress Tree
Foliage Colors
Dark 193
Medium 189
Light 190
Trunk Colors
Bark (Fibrous/scaly)
Basic 208
Secondary 208 + 217
Dark 217
Light 215
Dogwood Tree (Flowering)
Foliage Colors
Dark 194
Medium 195
Light 190
Trunk Colors
Bark (Scaly bumps)
Basic 220
Secondary 220 + 219
Dark 219
Light 221
Blossom, Pink 64
White 108, 130
Elm Tree (American)
Foliage Colors
Dark 226
Medium 227
Light 229
Trunk Colors
Bark (Vertical ridges)
Basic 210
Secondary 210 + 216
Dark 216
Light 209
Eucalyptus Tree
Foliage Colors (General)
Dark 177
Medium 176
Light 179
Bronze Green 233, 234
Reddish Leaf Color 235
Trunk Colors
Bark (Peeling strips)
Basic 180 & 184
Secondary 180 + 181
Dark 182 & 183
Light Tan 181
Fir Tree (Douglas)
Foliage Colors
Dark 194
Medium 195
Light 196
Trunk Colors
Bark (Thick, furrowed)
Basic 220
Secondary 220 + 216
Dark 216
Light 208
Hemlock Tree
Foliage Colors
Dark 186
Medium 187
Light 199
Trunk Colors
Bark (Deep furrowed scales)
Basic 213
Secondary 213 + 219
Dark 219
Light 218
Hickory Tree (Black)
Foliage Colors
Dark 188
Medium 202
Light 201
Trunk Colors
Bark (Deep furrows)
Basic 211
Secondary 211 + 222
Dark 222
Light Spots 209
Holly Tree (American)
Foliage Colors
Dark 225
Medium 226
Light 229
Trunk Colors
Bark (Thin, Gray, variety of bumps)
Basic 211
Secondary 211 + 216

LEGEND

\+ Mix listed recipe colors together for one resultant color
& Use all listed color mixes individually on the scene
, Multiple recipes separated by a comma indicates a variation of selections

ColorGuidanceIndex

LEGEND

\+ Mix listed recipe colors together for one resultant color
& Use all listed color mixes individually on the scene
, Multiple recipes separated by a comma indicates a variation of selections

LEGEND

\+ Mix listed recipe colors together for one resultant color
& Use all listed color mixes individually on the scene
, Multiple recipes separated by a comma indicates a variation of selections

Y

About the Author

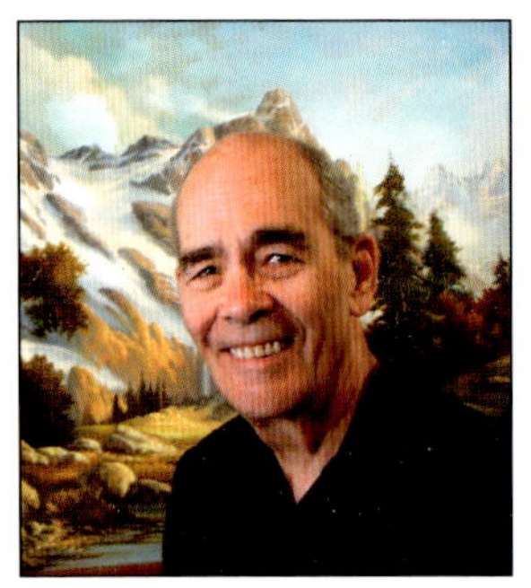

William F. Powell is an internationally recognized artist and one of America's foremost colorists. A native of Huntington, West Virginia, Bill studied at the Art Student's Career School in New York; Harrow Technical College in Harrow, England; and the Louvre Free School of Art in Paris, France. He has been professionally involved in fine art, commercial art, and technical illustrations for more than 45 years. His experience as an art instructor includes oil, watercolor, acrylic, colored pencil, and pastel—with subjects ranging from landscapes to portraits and wildlife. He also has authored a number of art instruction books including several popular Walter Foster titles. As a renowned master of color, Bill has conducted numerous "Color Mixing and Theory" workshops in various cities throughout the U.S. His expertise in color theory also led him to author and illustrate several articles and an educational series of 11 articles entitled "Color in Perspective" for a national art magazine. Bill also has performed as an art consultant for national space programs and for several artists' paint manufacturers. His work has included the creation of background sets for films, model making, animated cartoons, and animated films for computer mockup programs. He also produces instructional painting, color mixing, and drawing art videos.